Collaboration Design

Collaboration Design

A Step-by-Step Guide to Successful Collaboration

Mark Elliott

First published in 2019 by Starling Books,
an imprint of Collabforge Pty Ltd, Melbourne, Australia

Cover and text design by Peter Long
Typeset by Rebecca Dahl
Printed in Australia by IngramSpark

A catalogue record for this book is available from the National Library of Australia

9780648439820 (hardback)
9780648439837 (paperback)
9780648439844 (ebook)

To Keri
Cedar, Lucas, Jasper, River

I'm so grateful to be building this wild ride with you,
even as we ride it.

Table of Contents

Introduction

You can't avoid collaboration. The term appears in most corporate strategies, political speeches, government policies and community initiatives. From organisational transformation and international relations to climate change and the elimination of poverty, the concept has become the panacea for just about everything that falls into the too-hard basket. If only we could collaborate, we could solve ... [insert your wicked problem of choicc here].

Not only is collaboration popping up everywhere as a kind of all-purpose fix-it, it's used interchangeably with a whole slew of closely related terms: cooperation, codesign, communication, cocreation, user-centred design, design thinking, innovation, deliberation, agile development, even social media.

So why is everyone talking about collaboration, and what does it really mean?

The world we live in is becoming more complex and interconnected by the day. As we literally wire everything and everybody up to everything and everyone else, we are producing vast amounts of new information, understandings, perspectives, opportunities and issues. This is making it more and more difficult to get anything done without impacting others. We are creating the need for more collaboration simply by creating the modern world.

But while we may be forcing ourselves into more collaboration, the flipside of this is that collaboration done well can deliver truly great results. Genuine collaboration creates a sense of shared ownership, inspiring those involved to achieve higher levels of participation and productivity.

For government, successfully involving stakeholders in policy creation is more likely to result in 'voluntary compliance', reducing the need for monitoring, regulation and policing. For businesses, collaboration represents an opportunity for innovation by creating joint ventures, connecting internal units, and codesigning products and services with customers for a hand-in-glove fit. For not-for-profits and community organisations, collaboration can improve volunteer retention and deliver more impact through broader, better participation.

In general, products, services, programs, policies and strategies that are produced through genuine collaboration have the potential to actually be *better* than if they are developed by a small, closed group. They are more likely to address the needs of their users and to be promoted by those involved. This is extremely powerful because people trust the voices of their peers over the urgings of an organisation. And as we all know, those who write the plan don't fight the plan – it's a rare person who wants to see their own creation fail.

But here's the rub: the biggest challenge in converting this promise into reality is that, while I might feel I know what collaboration means, and so might you, *we* don't. As a society, we haven't yet developed widely shared understandings and methods for how to go about it. Rather, as individuals, we generally assume that others hold the same views regarding collaboration as we do. In reality, if you ask any two people what they think collaboration means for a specific situation, they'll typically tell you quite different things. This causes problems down the track when collaborators discover that they each have different expectations, or that they haven't actually agreed on how they'll work together. This means that successful collaboration in professional environments often comes down to whether or not you happen to be lucky enough to be working with someone who also shares your collaboration approaches, ideas and experiences.

The fact that we find ourselves in this position is actually quite understandable. Everyone, in every culture, collaborates on every topic imaginable. So it's reasonable to think that the ability to collaborate well is simply in our DNA. This unspoken assumption dominates the thinking in organisations of every type: we should be able to throw together a team at a moment's notice, and as part of their collective professional capability, they should be able to immediately collaborate and produce high-quality outcomes. But this simply isn't true. Each new collaboration is confronted by a *capability curve*: all collaborating groups perform with less capability at the outset but improve as they cocreate a shared culture and practice.

There is an upside to this unreasonable expectation. We, that is humanity, have a *huge* opportunity to improve our work together! By creating and sharing great methods of collaboration, we can dramatically increase the reliability and efficacy of the efforts we make to address our greatest challenges. And it's not crazy to think that this can happen, because it already happens, all the time. We have a track record of suddenly becoming aware of a pattern of activity that needs formalising in order for us to reach our greatest potential, and just getting on with this.

As a simple example, consider project management, a discipline often confused with – and inappropriately applied to – collaborative projects. It was not that long ago historically speaking, in the 1950s, that some very smart people began to recognise that there was a particular pattern of work in organisations that was consistent, and that would benefit from a structured approach. Nowadays, there are so many different project management methods that it's not uncommon to hear someone ask a question like, 'Do you use PRINCE2 or Agile?' My dream is to live in a world where we ask a similar question about collaboration, a world where there's a range of collaborative approaches suited to different types of settings and desired outcomes.

Contributing one such method is exactly the purpose of this book. The approach presented here had its genesis in a PhD I completed some 15 years ago and has been refined through a decade of application at my company, Collabforge. It has been the basis for delivering over 500 projects with governments and public-sector bodies.

Throughout this journey of practice, learning and hard-won experience, my team and I have come to believe that great collaboration is something that can and should be designed. We also believe that the capability to do this, and to effectively carry out collaboration, is something that can readily be learned. To support this, we have developed techniques that rely on specific ways of understanding and doing collaboration – ways that are relatively easy to grasp and apply, and when done well, deliver immediate and consistent results.

The Collabforge method has the following simple structure.

Three principles pull together the core elements of a general theory of collaboration: the basis for understanding how collaboration works in all contexts, at all scales, in every culture around the world. These principles underpin our entire methodology and will be revisited throughout this book.

Six stages provide a guide for how any collaboration will unfold through time, as well as a framework for understanding where to focus your efforts at different points in this process. These stages are grounded in the three principles and will help you understand what challenges you should expect and how to deal with them.

Part II dedicates a chapter to each of the stages of collaboration:

1 Decide – how to make a conscious decision about whether or not to collaborate

2 Convene – how to bring people together and establish the conditions for cocreation
3 Cocreate – how to get people creating together in a variety of settings and conditions
4 Resolve – how to work through the tensions and challenges that will arise
5 Maintain – how to maintain momentum and keep participants interested and engaged
6 Grow – how to involve more people while maintaining focus and momentum

Finally, the 36 *tools* are the best practical techniques we've discovered and developed over the years at Collabforge. These tools represent the means of delivering our collaboration method, and they require no previous skills or experience to apply. Each tool is presented within the stage most relevant to it in Part II.

I've worked hard with my team to present this knowledge to you in a format that will be easy to engage with and straightforward to apply, irrespective of where you are in your collaboration journey. Whether you're a practitioner looking for an injection of skills and knowledge, or just interested to see what improving your collaboration capability might do for your prospects, this book should give you what you need.

Part I

Understanding Collaboration

CHAPTER 1

What Collaboration Isn't

Another Buzzword

Collaboration has become a bit of a buzzword of late, especially among our leaders. Its increasing appearance in government policies, political speeches and corporate strategies conjures up a particular ethos or intention – a *vibe*, if you like – of people working together closely and genuinely. However, its use in these contexts typically falls short of any specific meaning or definition. This is because those who use the word rely on an assumed shared understanding of it.

When using a well-known word, it's reasonable to expect others to understand what you mean. It's also reasonable to want to signal a particular intention or value set in regard to working with others. However, things break down with the assumption that invoking the word 'collaboration' is enough for everyone to know how to get it done. Great outcomes can't be expected from collaboration after the mere mention of the word, no matter the gravitas of the speaker.

It may sound like I'm coming down hard on leaders, but the current situation regarding collaboration isn't really their fault. There simply aren't robust frameworks and methods of collaboration that leaders can easily reference or adopt – although addressing this problem is precisely the purpose of this book.

Genuine, impactful collaboration also requires leaders to put themselves in situations where they can't always control the other participants, much less the outcomes. And leaders must be willing to admit that they don't have all the answers, which can be especially difficult for them – not just because the psychological make-up of the average executive, politician or entrepreneur compels them to lead forcefully, but also because of what we expect from them. We often exalt these folks, putting them on a pedestal and having very high expectations of them. In essence, we reinforce the need for leaders to be non-collaborative. We look to them to cut through, take charge, be bold, push ahead.

So while I do believe that leaders need to adopt a more nuanced perspective when they speak about collaboration, I would say the same goes for the rest of us too.

When specific and important results are expected from collaboration, the term itself needs explicit definition. Further, when collaborative participation is not voluntary – such as when a chief executive officer (CEO) delivers a collaboration mandate – then people can feel forced into it, ultimately giving far less to the process than if they'd felt part of the original decision. If leaders expect genuine collaboration, then they need to lead by example, acting collaboratively when building the case for collaboration.

Let's stop using collaboration as a buzzword. Instead, explain what you mean when you say it and involve others in the discussion. Remember that genuine collaboration is something we do *with* other people, not something we *tell* them to do.

The Command-and-Control Mindset

One of the most challenging aspects of collaboration is that it requires a certain mindset. Unfortunately, this mindset doesn't come naturally to everyone, despite all of us having had collaborative experiences – just because everyone eats doesn't mean that we're all great cooks.

Rather, it's something most of us have to work at. Even after having spent more than 30 years as a collaborative musician, and the last 10 years running a collaboration business, I regularly find myself needing to refine and improve my mindset, certainly as much as I develop my skill set. I'm constantly surprised by the nuances involved when collaborating with different people in different settings.

For example, I've recently had some fun putting together a band with other parents who live in my neighbourhood. Some of them were at one time professional musicians who gigged with the greats, while others have dreamed about being in a rock band since high school. But having not rehearsed with a band for a decade – since Collabforge and four kids took over my life! – I've found that my mindset has been retrained by hundreds of government collaboration projects, and that it isn't quite right for the highly informal and personal nature of band collaboration. Things got a little awkward when I suggested formal collaboration processes during rehearsals, which was hard to avoid doing because of my mindset.

So mindset matters, but one often applied (incorrectly) to collaboration I characterise as *command-and-control*. It's transactional and design-and-deliver in nature. Those with this mindset position themselves above or outside the need for collaboration. They tend to focus on establishing the parameters, mechanisms and incentives for collaboration, while not actually collaborating themselves. They think along the lines of: 'It's my role to make sure things get done, and done right ... I need to keep people on track'. But this view can kill the spirit of great collaboration, and in turn the potential for great outcomes.

The shift from a command-and-control mindset to one more suited to collaboration starts with *open listening* – really hearing what others are saying and taking on board their needs and interests. It focuses on helping the participants to feel secure, thereby inspiring them to share more freely. It cultivates a deeper appreciation for the personal interests and approaches of those involved, not just the subject matter at hand. Of course, this is easier said than done if the culture you work within is strongly hierarchical. In this kind of setting, it will take a fair amount of work for all involved to cultivate mindsets that encourage better collaboration. Fortunately, the Collabforge method, detailed in Part II of this book, is designed to help you make this change.

Confusing Technology with Collaboration

A collaborative mindset means recognising the importance of good communication, and the fact that hard work goes into achieving it. Effective communication involves the obvious things like style, tone and clarity of message, but equally important are the channels that we choose for different situations. A presentation, phone call, email or face-to-face chat can all deliver the same message, yet have a considerably different impact on those involved. This is especially true when you consider the role of technology in any given collaborative initiative. Throughout this book, I will talk about how to make the most of technology, but there's one point I want to make loud and clear up-front: collaboration is not a software tool.

Software can support and even enable collaboration. But a specific technology, no matter how advanced, successful in other contexts, perfect its features, or generally whiz-bang, will *not* in and of itself guarantee that collaboration will happen, let alone happen well. As you'll discover in later chapters, how particular groups go about adopting technology is a complex process – interestingly, one that mirrors many of the dynamics of how participants adopt collaboration initiatives. Social proof, which is the proof that comes from seeing your peers adopt or advocate something, is the primary driver for both collaboration and the technologies that support it.

Another mischaracterisation is that file-sharing equals collaboration, which is akin to saying that an intranet is the only collaboration tool an organisation needs. File-sharing can streamline collaboration, even make it possible in some cases. But peers sharing files doesn't equal collaboration. Files get shared for a great many reasons, only some of which are collaborative in nature. In fact, files can be shared for quite anti-collaborative reasons, such as stealing or leaking information, or exposing someone's failings. Similarly, intranets support any number of organisational needs, with collaboration being only one of them.

A parallel issue here is how we're beginning to rethink the structure of the physical spaces we work in, so as to have a more positive effect on collaborative outcomes. There is a related and growing trend that goes by a variety of names, such as 'hot-desking', 'open-plan offices', 'activity-based work environments' and 'co-working'. The basic principle is that more-open and mixed working environments will lead to more-productive interpersonal collisions and serendipitous meetings, which in turn will result in collaboration. But like the use of technology to support collaborative interactions, co-working and hot-desking are not collaboration – they will not guarantee that you work well with others, or work with others at all.

Avoiding C-Washing

Bringing about great collaboration means paying attention to a range of design and interaction considerations, which we'll explore in later chapters. But above all, consciously designing the appropriate conditions, settings and technologies for collaboration requires a specific and shared understanding of what collaboration is.

Meaningless or dishonest environmental commitments are known as *greenwashing*. Use of the term 'collaboration' in high-level policy and strategy contexts without any substantiation of how it will be enacted, I call *c-washing*. Like environmental impact and corporate social responsibility, when addressing organisational policy and strategy, leaders can find themselves mouthing what's clearly the right thing to say, but with little associated substance or a sincere intention to back it up.

Espousing collaboration in this way, empty of specific meaning and intent, will do little for you or your organisation. It's far more likely to cause problems by setting false expectations. Instead, rally yourself and your prospective collaborators around a shared belief regarding the value that collaboration represents. The following chapter gives you a starting point for doing this.

CHAPTER 2

What Collaboration Is

A Working Definition

So what, then, is collaboration? The answer depends on how you're coming at the concept. For example, it can be a noun: 'That collaboration was amazing'. This usage emphasises outcomes and experience. And then there's the verb: 'Shall we collaborate on that?' This puts the focus more on process. There's also the adjective: 'That wasn't very collaborative'. This stresses a quality or way of being with others. Putting each of these three lenses over collaboration helps us to see its different dimensions, while putting them all together provides us with a holistic view: collaboration delivers outcomes and experiences through processes that are characterised by a particular way of being with others.

Understanding and exploring all of the dimensions of collaboration has led me and my team to the method presented in Part II. The foundational concept of the Collabforge method is that, while there are many aspects and interpretations of collaboration, fundamentally, it happens when participants together create shared understandings and ideas that enable the realisation of an outcome.

These shared ideas may be plans, the recognition of pre-existing notions, interpretations of something newly encountered, or genuinely novel concepts. Regardless, the ideas must be jointly held prior to any outcome being pursued. As a result, the group must go through a process that plants the same 'idea seeds' in the minds of those involved. This process must also cultivate, validate and grow these ideas as they continue to be jointly held in the minds of the participants.

For example, let's imagine you and I are sitting together during an engaging presentation at a conference. Afterwards we strike up a conversation, during which you draw my attention to aspects of the presentation I hadn't thought about, helping me to confirm what it was that I liked so much about what was discussed. At the same time, you help me to see positives in some of the elements that I was critical of. At this point, we both spot the presenter leaving the stage and decide to talk to her. You and I relate to the speaker our opinions and interpretations from a shared perspective, both of us on the same page with a nuanced understanding of the presentation. This shared understanding provides a platform for the presenter to respond, enriching my ideas and understandings as well as yours through clarifications and further background. Over the course of another five or 10 minutes, the platform that was initially an understanding shared between you and me, continues to expand until it includes the speaker's perspectives and ideas as well.

This scenario is a very simplistic example of collaboration, but it draws out the key elements: the mindset (being open-minded as we all discuss ideas of interest), the process (turn-taking in a conversation that progressively involves more participants) and the outcome (a jointly held interpretation of a presentation, one that exemplifies a greater depth of understanding than any individual perspective).

Expanding this little story, perhaps the three of us (you, me and the presenter) get excited by the prospect of sharing our jointly held ideas with more people. I say that I have a few clients who would benefit from seeing the presentation, and you mention a working group that would love it too. We then settle on the three of us having lunch together to continue turning over these ideas, to see what we can make happen. This brings into play the cocreation of a shared plan and outcome.

Consolidating these elements gives us the fundamental arc of collaboration (see Figure 1), as well as a working definition of the term:

A shared understanding enabling a shared vision, followed by a plan that supports the realisation of an outcome.

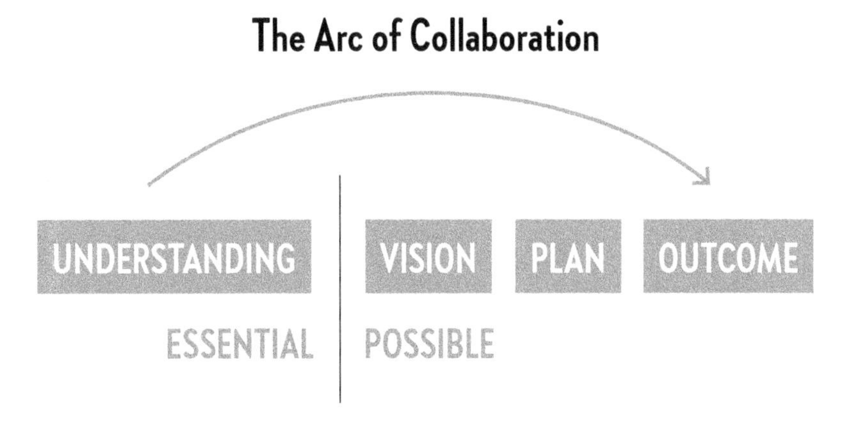

Figure 1. The Arc of Collaboration

Of course, you may not choose to, or be able to, progress through all of these steps, but to greater or lesser degrees, they are all required for genuine collaboration to take place.

Cocreation

At the heart of genuine, real or authentic collaboration – however you might characterise collaboration that goes beyond being a buzzword or simply 'working together' – sits the notion of *cocreation*, or put more plainly, people creating something together. This 'something' is, at its root, always an idea. That is, the cocreation must exist first and foremost at the level of ideas. Even if the thing to be created is a physical object, it must first exist as a conceptual representation in the minds of the creators. This nuance is very important. As we'll see in Chapter 6, where we explore cocreation in more detail, it points to the key requirements for getting collaboration to not just work, but work well. The cocreation of jointly held ideas is the minimum requirement for effective collaboration.

Interestingly, the notion that collaboration is dependent on cocreation accords with the origins of the term. The word 'collaborator' first appeared in print in 1802 and is attributed to the English philosopher and political radical Jeremy Bentham.[1] In this first recorded usage of the term, Bentham described the activity of those *co-authoring* scientific papers together. In 1860, a variation of the term with the suffix '-ion' appeared in a published work by the English novelist Charles Reade, who noted when referring to co-authoring playwrights that '[o]n the French stage, collaboration has lately become quite common'.[2]

It would appear that the original use of the word 'collaboration' in the English language was intended to describe instances where multiple creators contributed to a single cocreated output, such as a scientific paper or the script for a play. This subtle focus on cocreation distinguishes collaboration from the older related term *cooperation*.

The history and definition of cooperation reflect the simple concept of working together towards a common end or purpose, but without creative outputs coming into the picture. Early definitions and usage of cooperation weren't specifically focused on multiple individuals

---

1 Bentham is well remembered for a number of forward-looking philosophical contributions. These include advocating animal rights, the easing of laws prohibiting same-sex attraction, contributions to the philosophical branch of utilitarianism, and the design of the panopticon prison. See University College London, 'Bentham Project', 2019, https://www.ucl.ac.uk/bentham-project

2 'Collaboration', in JA Simpson and ESC Weiner (eds), *Oxford English Dictionary*, 2nd edn, Oxford University Press, Oxford, 1989.

creating something like a play or scientific publication together. Here, the *work* aspect of working together was emphasised over the creative outputs. This suggests the more-pragmatic type of interaction often implied by the term 'cooperation' today.

For example, you and I might engage in cooperation if you were to provide me with a brief for building a new deck in your backyard, based on *your* specifications for the design, materials and budget. My job would to deliver the deck according to your specs, with you providing feedback and oversight. When trying to distinguish cooperation from cocreation, it's helpful to consider the former as being transactional and more in line with the command-and-control mindset discussed in Chapter 1.

Interestingly, having designed and delivered hundreds of collaborations, I've discovered that it's when cocreation is strategically focused, well resourced and supported by cooperation, that the real magic of collaboration happens. Not only does this prompt truly shared plans and outcomes to emerge, it also enables a collaboration to scale more easily beyond its instigators. We will further discuss the interrelationship between cocreation and cooperation in Chapter 6, where we'll see how both processes contribute to a more holistic view of collaboration.

The Improvisation Mindset

The *magic* that comes from getting the right blend of cocreation and cooperation during collaboration is that it accelerates the generation of emergent outcomes; that is, the unpredictable outcomes that arise through complex interactions. It can be disconcerting when these outcomes come at you quickly. You may be put on the spot, having to consider options you thought might not come about so soon, or at all. This need to react to the unexpected is very much akin to improvisation.

Imagine taking part in an improvised play where the participants are free to create their own dialogue, once the characters and high-level plot direction are established. You'll need to think on your feet, to be creative with both your responses and behaviours in the moment, as well as with where you guide your character and the storyline, regarding the overall dramatic arc of the play. That's a lot to think about! Watching skilled improv performers in any artistic field is a magical experience. You're drawn in by the added layer of tension as they bring spontaneity and creativity to their reactions, especially when you remember that they have no 'script' to fall back on.

This is exactly what happens in any collaboration: you set up a situation or scenario with generalised parameters and then press 'Go'. It's why collaboration can be so dynamic and enjoyable as an experience, but also so challenging. There are a great many factors to keep in mind as you make on-the-spot decisions that may have far-reaching, long-term consequences.

That said, to keep things in perspective, it's worth remembering that larger collaborations are always comprised of many smaller sub-collaborations that provide ample opportunities for course correction. It's also important to cultivate the collaborative norm that it's OK to slow down, or even pause to reflect, before making big decisions. Part II will provide you with many techniques for doing this, and for making high-quality collaborative decisions in general. The main thing to keep in mind at this point is that the more you achieve a fluid and relaxed improvisation with your fellow participants, the more efficient your collaboration will be.

Communication Feedback Loops

Communication channels are one of the primary means for a collaborative group to create and close the feedback loop that pushes it forward. This sounds obvious, but it's surprising how often collaborative projects are established with too few or insufficient communication channels. When participants are properly immersed and inspired, ideas can arise at any time. How quickly they can respond to each other will drive the generation of outcomes.

For example, just imagine that you and I have a face-to-face conversation where you ask me a question. However, not only do I not look you in the eyes while you talk, I don't even turn to face you, and I don't bother replying until the following day. Imagine the effect that this behaviour will have. Things won't get very far very fast, and the whole thing certainly won't be very engaging! This little hypothetical is essentially what happens when you use email as your primary collaborative communication channel – timelines stretch out and energy drains from the interactions.

Of course, we don't usually have the luxury of being physically present with our collaborators 24/7 (nor would we want to!), but we don't need to be, as a wide range of communication and collaboration tools are now freely available. The members of my band adopted the mobile messaging application WhatsApp to coordinate carpooling for getting to rehearsals, and other logistics. Once we all got the hang of it, we quickly extended its use to many other, more creative matters. The highly interactive nature of instant messaging drove many lively conversations between the band members, which in turn fuelled our energy and inspiration.

The big takeaway here is that regular, easy and responsive communication is essential for creating the positive feedback loops that drive collaboration. In addition, technology will likely enable any collaboration that extends beyond face-to-face interactions. Now, it can be challenging, if not impossible, to predict which technology will be an ideal fit for a group, until the members of the group have conducted their own trials. And as many of us know from our professional working environments, we don't always have the opportunity to select the communication tools we most want to use. The good news is that the likelihood of a group adopting a technology that enables positive feedback can be greatly increased using the methods spelt out in Chapter 8 for convening an initiative – the second stage of collaboration.

Genuine Collaboration

However you achieve it, regular, high-quality communication is required in collaboration in order to build a shared understanding. This communication sets in motion an interplay of ideas and interactions that ultimately require some improvisation as the participants respond and cocreate new ideas. If these ideas are compelling, your group will be moved to action, leading to the realisation of outcomes. This is collaboration. You'll certainly recognise this process – it would be very rare for a person to never have had a genuine collaborative experience! But you'll also be familiar with less-productive collaborative experiences. The next chapter looks at why this is the case.

CHAPTER 3

Why Collaboration Often Falls Short

Collaboration Killers

When I ask people how many of their collaborative experiences have lived up to expectations, most reply that the majority have not. I wonder if this is true for you. That this might be the norm is a shame, but it's also to be expected. Part of the reason for this is the previously discussed lack of agreed, best-practice methods for achieving it – although this book gives it a shot! However, there are other reasons for why a collaboration may not fulfil its promise that are surprisingly simple, and if you're aware of them, they can easily be avoided.

One of the most common collaboration killers is unrealistic expectations regarding the time and effort required. People kick off a collaboration all fired up about what they can do as a group, boosting each other's excitement, and often their egos too. This fire tends to be fuelled by lively conversation and the sparks that fly when new relationships are forged. But it soon burns out, once you settle into a daily grind and get a clearer picture of your group's actual commitment and capability. Temper your initial enthusiasm with the expectation that the process will inevitably be harder and slower than you anticipate – this will prepare you for the long haul.

Another collaboration killer is not allowing enough time and space for the necessary capability to be built at the outset. As a general rule, collaborative capability needs to be built afresh for each new group and each new project, which means it will take time to gain momentum. In other words, when you begin a new collaborative project, you have to slow things right down so that you can speed up later. This can be a bitter pill to swallow if you're time-poor and used to doing things alone or in more-cooperative modes. Nevertheless, it's essential that you remember this point: your participants will simply need time working together to reach their full potential. In fact, this is a key part of the third principle of collaboration – shared capability – which is outlined in Chapter 6.

Another thing that can destroy a collaboration before it even gets going is trying to involve too many participants too early in the process. Collaboration doesn't scale easily, which is especially true at the outset. Until a group has built a strong shared practice, its members will be very susceptible to negative social dynamics as they look to one another for social proof. After the start-up sparks fade and the going gets tougher, there can be a mass exodus. So take it slowly when looking to introduce more members. Chapter 12 is dedicated to helping you successfully navigate the challenges of growth – the sixth stage of collaboration.

A further early-stage collaboration challenge, especially in organisational settings, is when, having set the direction with an opening speech or participated in a kick-off meeting, leadership departs, thinking their job is now done. This sends a signal to others that now is the time to back out if you're important, leaving the grunt work to lesser beings – and, of course, we all want to feel that we're important. Needless to say, be very conscious of the signals that you or your leadership send out during the early stages of a collaboration, or you may end up losing participants you desperately need.

As I explained in Chapter 1, leaders also need to be aware that these initial stages can be especially uncomfortable if they're genuine about participating. The collaborative mindset requires them to be open and, to some degree, vulnerable. Further, early collaborative conversations are often shaky, unclear, and slowed by numerous digressions and questions – precisely the opposite of the fast-paced, decisive approach many leaders are used to taking. These dynamics often result in leaders unconsciously shutting down these important conversations in an attempt to drive efficiency or avoid discomfort, stunting the growth of the group's collaborative capability and hampering its ability to deliver an outcome. If you're a leader, or you have the ear of one, simply raising these issues can go a long way towards resolving them.

We'll look at how to better involve leaders in collaboration in Chapter 7, which discusses how to make the initial decision to work together (the first stage of collaboration), and in Chapter 11, which explains how to maintain collaboration (the fifth stage). For now, just remember that a slow start is a normal, even important part of collaboration, and that greater benefits will flow from being patient and fully involved from the outset.

Blind Spots

Many collaboration killers are due to blind spots that we can have as individuals and as groups. We're all capable of a remarkable inability to recognise specific gaps or deficiencies in our plans or expectations. I consider this to be a natural consequence of being human.

Did you know that there's a literal blind spot in the human eye, precisely where our optic nerve connects to our retina? The very attribute that gives us sight also creates blindness! If you've never tried it before, have a go at the following. Holding this book at about arm's length from your face, close or cover your left eye and stare at the cross in Figure 2 (see the next page) with your right eye. Now slowly move the book towards your face.

When the book is about 30 centimetres away, the black spot in Figure 2 will disappear as it aligns with your retinal-nerve blind spot.

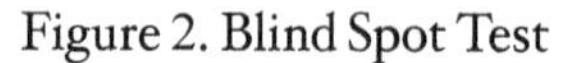

Figure 2. Blind Spot Test

In fact, a big case that I'm putting forward in this book is that our global society has a massive blind spot in regard to collaboration. We're often blind to what causes collaboration to fail, in addition to only vaguely perceiving what it is, how it works and why we do it.

Fortunately, there are some useful approaches to identifying blind spots. Zooming in and out to different scales can help. For example, if you've been exclusively focused on the needs and interests of your core team of collaborators, you may have neglected the needs and interests of those in your 'authorising environment'. This is a very common issue that can end with a team presenting its results to the CEO, only to find out that it has completely missed the mark and won't be getting another crack at it.

Another approach is to get feedback on your plans and expectations from friends who are different enough from you that they have different blind spots. You should trust these friends to tell you straight up what they think, including what your blind spots might be. (Though don't expect an entirely honest assessment from anyone who has a serious vested interest in your collaborative venture!) Now you have to listen openly and really hear what your friends are telling you – which can be the hardest part.

Next, I discuss some blind spots that are among the most common challenges Collabforge has encountered over the last decade: the missing chair (lack of a common understanding of collaboration), the missing team (insufficient shared capability) and the missing elephant (no common culture, processes or tools). I also talk about some issues concerning settings and tools that may lead you astray. Our method, presented in Part II, will help you to address each of these.

The Missing Chair

As I mentioned in the introduction to this book, you and I each know what collaboration means, but we – much like society as a whole on this topic – are unlikely to be in agreement. This is a gap in our shared understanding regarding how we define the word. Because collaboration seems to be in our DNA, we've been fooled into thinking that there's a common reference point all of us can rely on – a one-size-fits-all *chair* we can each sit in when we need to. But because there are no broadly accepted definitions or methodologies that we can make safe assumptions about, like there are in project management, we all fall on our rear ends when we try to sit in this missing chair.

The Missing Team

Collaboration is akin to a team sport, and all great teams build their capability collectively. No-one would expect a team to win a match without the players having ever practised together, yet organisations regularly form new teams to tackle new challenges without resourcing any such practice. We seem to expect business professionals to be competent collaborators straight out of the gate, their productivity occurring automatically, but this simply isn't true. Everyone needs to practise passing and catching a ball before they can be relied on not to drop it. Collaborative teams need to be able to test and agree on ways of working – specific processes, tools and technologies – in addition to doing 'the real work' of delivering the outputs of collaboration.

The Missing Elephant

To get their work done, collaboratively or otherwise, organisations tend to rely on an often sizeable, always complex integration of culture, processes and tools – an *elephant*, if you will, that their staff can ride. As a result, when an organisation collaborates with another organisation, or even across significantly different parts of the same business, the implicit question is always, 'Will we ride your elephant or mine?' And therein lies the problem: no-one really wants to get down off their own elephant and climb onto someone else's unfamiliar and possibly cantankerous beast. When a new elephant is needed – a new set of shared culture, tools and processes – procuring one can be expensive, time-consuming and risky: the equivalent of launching and managing an elephant-breeding program! Even the task of deciding who will take on these risks and costs can kill a collaboration before it begins.

Understanding Your Setting

Different collaborative settings that require different approaches comprise another blind spot. For example, early in my career as a collaboration designer, I would come home from work all excited about a new method or technique, and I'd try to apply it to my domestic circumstances. Similar to my experiences with my band, I quickly learned that the highly structured methods that work well in meeting rooms with business teams can be too formal to work well at the kitchen table with family members. They just feel too mechanical to contribute to that feeling of relaxed enjoyment that you want with your own flesh and blood.

Work versus home are just two of many collaborative settings, and experience has taught me that there aren't always solid lines differentiating one setting from another. So it's important to be conscious of collaborative settings that are different to what you're used to, or to which you may be blindly applying ill-suited methods. When this is the case, when you realise that you're not getting the results you want, be ready with your improvisation mindset to adapt and try a different approach.

Tech Tool Trouble

Yet another blind spot I've encountered is the expectation that a technological tool will solve a collaboration problem. This assumption often arises in those interested in a particular technology, or those who've had some success with specific technology in another setting. It usually manifests in a version of the statement, 'If only people would adopt X tool, then we could really get things done!' But while this might be valid, it's almost never an easy or realistic expectation to place on a group. As I mentioned earlier, not only is technology adoption a very complex if not illogical process in itself, if a group faces a particular issue, this can often be replicated, even exacerbated, by technology.

I'll talk more about how to properly introduce collaboration technologies in Chapter 8, on convening collaboration (the second stage of the process), and Chapter 12, on growing collaboration (the sixth stage), but in the meantime, the best advice I can give you on this front, as I mentioned at the start of this chapter, is to go slowly. Take some time to think about and discuss with others the barriers and challenges that people are experiencing with a particular technology. Create situations where you can test a particular tool before you commit to using it. Once you've made your choice, locate or strive to be a model user who can clearly demonstrate the value of the tool to others. Above all, listen to and support those who may be struggling. And be aware that the biggest signal you're likely to get that people aren't into a particular technology, is no signal at all.

Taking a thoughtful, even a careful approach to technology is necessary because regardless of the scale or subject matter, your collaboration will undoubtedly rely on it in some form or fashion. Whatever tech you use, remember that it's something that will be put *between* your participants, so you need to continuously strengthen your understanding of how technology can best support your desired outcomes, and how to sustain its adoption by the participants – if they don't sense it's needed or feel capable of using it, you may end up driving them apart.

The next chapter's simple but powerful *people, process and tools* framework will help you stay focused on the role of technology while balancing it out with key human factors.

CHAPTER 4

When Collaboration Succeeds

The Third Hand

When collaboration really works, it rings like a bell. Participants seem to have an almost psychic connection with one another, anticipating each other's needs and intentions without speaking. They automatically know how to get things done together, drawing on a shared history of successes and failures, breakthroughs and lessons learned. Their shared capability can become so strong that a new entity seems to arise from within the collaboration, from all the participants acting as one. It feels like a new contributor, but one that has the ability to do things that none of the individuals can do alone. This has been described as *the third hand*.[3]

When the third hand emerges, it's the result of alignment across three key domains: people, process and tools. While this framework is not new – there are literally hundreds of millions of references if you google 'people process tools' – it does provide a means of understanding the primary dimensions within which collaboration operates.

---

3 For more on this concept, and collaboration in art in general, see Charles Green, *The Third Hand: Collaboration in Art from Conceptualism to Postmodernism,* University of Minnesota Press, Minneapolis, 2001.

People

People encompasses a group's culture, values, norms and interpersonal skills. When the members of a group have had the time and opportunity to build up a set of experiences together, these naturally lend themselves to reinforcing a particular way of behaving. These behaviours often emerge without conscious thought on the part of the individuals in the group. If this doesn't happen, participants can feel distant from one another, and their interactions lifeless, mechanical and awkward.

If the collaboration is taking place within an organisation, much of this 'people' factor will already be in play. Ask yourself the following questions to make a quick assessment of how conducive your organisation's culture is to collaboration:

- When groups in your organisation get together, do they openly share information, ideas and experiences, in the interests of arriving at new and better understandings?
- Does your organisation prioritise respectful, open and honest communication?
- When new ideas emerge, especially those that challenge the status quo or the opinions of leadership, are they met with genuine interest?

If you answered 'Yes' to these questions, you should have a strong foundation for collaboration. If you answered 'No' to any of them, the method outlined in Part II should help you to address the challenges you face.

Process

Process has two key elements: social and business processes.

Social processes are the things people do that aren't mandated by an organisation and may even be done unconsciously. Simple norms such as holding a door open for someone or regularly taking lunch with your co-workers lie within the realm of organisational culture – normalised and expected behaviours that reinforce our connection with one another, but which don't necessarily add direct, quantifiable business value.

For example, at Collabforge we have a cultural norm of helping others to articulate something if, for some reason, people are not letting them. So in a group discussion, if a team member notices that someone else seems to have something to say but isn't getting the chance to say it, they might interrupt the flow of conversation to allow this person to speak. This social process acknowledges the fact that our capacity for communication can vary in different situations, and it helps ensure that everyone is heard.

Business processes, on the other hand, are things people do with a specific work or productivity objective in mind, and that are often (but not always) prescribed by an organisation. They include processes like taking a standard approach to storing files in an intranet, or following a particular project-management method. Business processes are often step-by-step ways of getting things done that staff are expected to comply with.

As an example, at Collabforge we have a business process for designing facilitated events. The first step is to explicitly clarify the outcome and impact the event should deliver for our client. Then, after listing any activities that have to take place (the *givens*, as we call them), we create a list of other activities that, based on our experience, will help deliver the defined outcome and impact. Once we've narrowed in on the activities that are necessary (the givens) and compelling (will deliver the outcome/impact), we plan each to the minute. We go to this level of detail to ensure we run to schedule – one of the more-challenging aspects of facilitation – and to help us think through the experiential, logistical and interpersonal complexities involved. Finally, we develop strategies for any *pivots* (deviations from the plan) we might need to make if an activity delivers a dramatically unexpected outcome.

The line between social and business processes can be fuzzy. Some years ago, we developed a simple technique that anyone can use to signal to a speaker that they have an idea they'd like to introduce into the discussion: simply pinching their thumb and middle finger together. This tells the speaker that they should pass on the 'talking stick' when they reach a natural break in the discussion. This technique helps maintain the flow of conversation, and interestingly, it also helps you remember the point you want to make, which you visualise holding between your thumb and middle finger.

Although this began as more of a social process at Collabforge, we now use it in client meetings to indicate to each another that we have something valuable to contribute. This subtle signal is almost never noticed by those who don't know to look for it, yet it has the effect of seamlessly coordinating our team members, allowing us to follow up and support each other's ideas in a way that can be extremely beneficial to the client. However, it's not exactly mandated, so it doesn't qualify as a full-blown business process.

Generally speaking, when it comes to designing business and social processes for collaboration, the social side is far more difficult than the business side. Social processes seem to best emerge organically, which takes time spent working together. But often we don't have a surplus of time, which pushes us into designing collaborative business processes at the outset of an initiative. And this can be a good approach if the business process is developed collaboratively with participants. But be wary of overdoing it. Too many step-by-step processes introduced too quickly can push people away from the improvisation mindset and make them feel too constrained. This can also limit the group's flexibility, and as a result, the ability to develop approaches that best suit the members' needs and personalities.

Tools

When it comes to the *tools* of collaboration, it's important to remember that these can be physical, digital or conceptual, and that these forms often work together. For example, when collaboratively writing a report, your group might turn to the physical tool of a computer, the digital software that runs on it, and conceptual templates for the report itself.

In choosing tools to support collaboration, most people focus on digital communication and document-sharing technologies. But while these are usually necessary, there's a range of other tools that should be considered. An inspiring workspace fitted out with quality whiteboards and projection gear can dramatically improve a face-to-face session. On the other hand, there are conceptual tools that can give a group's capability a shot in the arm – for example, the 36 tools presented in Part II of this book.

Like the people and process dimensions of collaboration, the design and selection of collaborative tools always benefit from group consideration. Even when choice isn't an option, such as when your organisation mandates a particular tool or technology, a discussion that draws out the participants' experiences, perceptions and knowledge can be of considerable help. A person in your group who has advanced skills in using a key tool can accelerate your collective capability. On the other hand, someone who has had a negative experience with a tool, or holds to a bad perception of it, can impede your group's progress by 'poisoning the well'. In both cases, early awareness and open discussions can make a big difference.

Early Preparation

Ultimately, people, process and tools are among the most important yet complex aspects of collaboration design – though how you consider, develop and maintain each of them is more of an art than a science. We'll dive into various techniques for embedding these crucial dimensions of collaboration in Part II.

For now, let's look at how an early focus on getting a good blend of people, process and tools can do much to encourage the emergence of the third hand.

In the 10 years since Collabforge was established, we've delivered a number of projects aimed at fixing collaborative issues that could have been avoided with more thought and discussion early on. When it comes to collaboration, it's smarter and less expensive to invest a little more time and work up-front than to put off dealing with any issues until later.

This is a theme that crops up throughout this book – slowing down at the start in order to speed up later. By beginning with open and honest conversations that focus on aspects such as personal interests, expected outcomes, past experiences, and roles and responsibilities, you create a strong foundation that will better support you in the later stages of collaboration. If you don't take the time to do this, issues can develop and fester, only to erupt at the worst possible moment. For example, while working on one collaborative event, I didn't take enough time to make sure the individuals in the group were clear on each other's roles and responsibilities. For various reasons, it didn't feel important to do at the time. However, it turned out to be important to someone else – a fact that would've been useful to discover at the outset. This person's frustration was suppressed in the early stages of the event, but nonetheless continued to grow, finally emerging at a critical juncture! While it didn't lead to a catastrophic breakdown of the collaboration, it certainly lowered the overall capability of the group and reduced the quality of the outcome.

This is such a common experience in collaboration that I've come to call it *ironing in wrinkles*. If you've done much clothes ironing, you've probably had the experience of erasing the creases on the top side of a garment, only to flip it over and see that you've unintentionally embedded new creases on the underside – ones that require considerably more ironing to remove than any naturally occurring wrinkle.

Moving too quickly at the start of a collaboration has the same effect. It can look like you're doing good work on the surface, ironing out wrinkles through discussions, workshopping and the like. But by ignoring the deeper issues, you've actually been *creating* wrinkles within your group's shared understanding and expectations.

Throughout the many projects we've conducted at Collabforge, we've found that the following five tenets stand out as those that best set up a collaboration for success from the very beginning. The expanded method in Part II of this book will help you ensure that these principles are addressed – including not ironing in any wrinkles!

RESOURCE COLLABORATION IN LINE WITH EXPECTATIONS

One of the best ways of getting off to a good start is to have access to the required resources – at the very beginning, when the collaboration capability is at its lowest. Ask yourself how much the outcomes from an initiative are dependent on great collaboration, in percentage terms, then use this percentage as an indicator of the level of resourcing you should commit to in establishing and supporting your collaborative capability. For example, if you feel that 50% of your initiative's outcomes are dependent on great collaboration, then consider investing 50% of your available resources into developing and delivering a great collaboration design. This is the first step in ensuring you'll have what you need to build up your people, processes and tools at the outset as well as throughout the project.

ESTABLISH COMMON GROUND

In these early stages, focus on creating common ground among the participants by discussing key terms, concepts and assumptions regarding ways of working, as well as processes, tools, and, of course, the expected outcomes and impact. Also consider discussing the topic of *collaborative culture*; specifically, what the term means to the individuals involved, and what might it mean for the endeavour that's on the table.

Don't shy away from challenging topics, or those that feel too simple or obvious. If they truly are too simple or obvious, you'll be able to move on quickly; if not, everyone will be thankful for the opportunity to discuss them, even if they weren't so sure to begin with.

PRACTISE WITHOUT PRESSURE

Create engaging, even fun opportunities for practising collaboration that are decoupled from delivery. For example, ask your group to build a LEGO prototype or model of your collaboration's imagined outcome – for details of this approach, refer to Tool 17: The LEGO Challenge. This is a great way of uncovering expectations, attitudes and experiences sooner rather than later, and it will likely solicit open and engaged dialogue.

Another great approach is to play a game as a group. There is any number of quick and easy card-based games that take about 10 minutes to play and that will generate lots of goodwill and opportunities for participants to practise working as a group.

MAINTAIN THE MOMENTUM

One of the biggest threats to collaborative initiatives is flagging momentum. This includes natural pauses in activity like vacations or personal leave, but it can also happen when enthusiasm fades and the reality of the long haul sinks in. Having a regular and facilitated rhythm of interaction is the key to maintaining your momentum and bridging these gaps.

Plan for this early on and work hard to make it happen. Establish up-front the expectation that a regular rhythm is to be a key part of participation, then make sure this actually comes about. The fifth stage of collaboration, maintaining it, as covered in Chapter 11, encompasses a range of tools for keeping your group focused and energised in order to maintain momentum and a regular pattern of activity.

DESIGN FOR GROWTH WHILE WELCOMING TENSION

Collaborations generate value by resolving tensions within groups. For example, shared value is created when a group arrives at a collective decision after considering a range of competing options proposed by different participants. Without the challenge of diverse ideas and approaches, groupthink will reign, and peer pressure and conformity will shut down the hard conversations. So it's essential to enter collaborations *expecting* a range of these tensions. At the same time, however, you need processes for resolving them. Chapter 10 provides a range of tools for resolving tension, while Chapter 12 is focused on key aspects of growth.

The Importance of Externalising

High-performing collaborative groups also develop quite a strong capability for what I call *externalising*: getting that which is in the minds of individual members of a group out into the collaboration environment. This could mean spelling out ideas in documents, emails and presentations, or on sticky notes or whiteboards. You might translate your ideas directly into a physical form if prototyping with clay or some other modelling material. You might even use waves of sound or body movements if your collaboration involves dance and music. No matter the medium, for all substantive collaborations, there will be the creation of some form of external *output*. This output will then enable the realisation of collaborative *outcomes*.

Up to this point, I've mainly used the word 'outcome' to describe the result of a collaboration. But it's useful to draw a distinction between outcomes and outputs, with outcomes describing the more abstract side of what collaboration delivers, and outputs describing the more tangible side. For example, an output might be a strategy document that your team has produced, describing why and how a specific change will happen in your organisation. The outcome, on the other hand, will be the understanding, alignment and buy-in that the strategy process produces. As this example makes clear, outcomes, *not* outputs, are typically the important impact that a collaboration is intended to make. This is why, throughout this book, I encourage you to stay focused on producing outcomes over outputs, especially as you design your collaboration.

That said, outputs are the primary means by which the understanding and vision shared within a group become tangible to the participants and the world around them. In other words, the progressive development by participants of the capability to cocreate outputs together is essential in motivating them, as well as validating that what they hold in their minds individually is actually shared with their peers. And perhaps even more importantly, outputs are the vehicle through which the ultimate goal, the outcomes, are realised. So you have to stay focused on ensuring your group remains productive with regard to outputs.

The simplest way to assess the production of outputs is to reflect on what your group has recently externalised, irrespective of the medium or activity. What was the last idea that the group got out of its collective head? Was it valuable to them? Did it help them to understand, improve or progress their efforts? If not, then your group has likely been spinning its wheels and being unproductive. If this happens to apply to you at the moment, fear not – the Collabforge method presented in Part II will give you exactly what you need to get things moving.

A challenge that often arises in the context of externalising and producing outputs is the unwitting creation of an *integration bottleneck,* when there's a failure to successfully synthesise all the great ideas and inputs from a large group into a single output. This typically happens when a single person takes on the difficult and frequently painful editorial role of amassing contributions, making sense of them, then adding them to the object of cocreation, whether this is a strategy, product or production. When an individual is saddled with this entire process, you risk damaging your collaboration.

A common example is a document shared by a group for review. Participants often make comments in the margins like 'Change this to that' or 'I think this point should be sharpened', assuming that someone else will make the suggested change for them. This might make sense in terms of ensuring there's a consistent *voice* across the document, but if there are many participants, it creates quite a workload for a single person. At Collabforge, we've found that it's far better to support and encourage participants to do their own integration, with an editorial review planned for later to embed that seamless voice. By distributing the responsibility of integration in this way, the individual contributions tend to be of higher quality, the understanding and vision are more deeply shared, and the group is more productive. To support this, we often introduce collaborative document-editing tools, along with simple norms and processes such as one person explaining any substantial edits to another's work.

This can all take a little getting used to if you've never worked this way before, but within a few weeks, the sheer efficiency of it will shine through. And if you can use live collaborative editing tools, there's also the excitement of seeing a document come together before your eyes – a living demonstration of how 'many hands make light work'.

Other key collective capabilities are encouraged when you get better at externalising, and when you create shared outputs through the efficient integration of contributions. Being able to review where your group left off in the last session, or what key decisions were made, is a simple but powerful means of supporting your group's collective memory. Externalising your group's thinking will also improve your ability to handle complexity; you'll find a great technique for this in Chapter 10 – Tool 25: Brainstorm, Bundle and Bind – the 3Bs. Clear outputs that communicate what your collaboration is all about will reduce the time and energy needed to onboard others. In many respects, this is what the second stage of the Collabforge method, convening collaboration, is all about (see Chapter 8).

As you continue reading, keep in mind that while externalising is inherent in most collaborations, doing it really well is absolutely essential for a great result. It will improve your productivity and your ability to tackle complex problems, and it will help you to grow your membership over time, if this is one of your goals. Building the skill and habit of effective externalisation is a central focus of the Collabforge method.

Success by Design

In Chapter 3, I introduced the idea of 'the missing team', a common blind spot in collaboration. I also mentioned how collaboration is akin to a team sport. That's because team sports are a fantastic example of all the elements of great collaboration coming together to drive success.

For at least 2000 years, going back to the Chinese football-style sport of cuju and the ancient Mayan ball game of pitz, humans have enjoyed an extraordinary capability to achieve high-performance results in sporting groups, be it teams playing basketball, soccer, cricket or other international or local favourites. Culture runs deep and strong through most sports teams, especially those whose ability and reputation is dependent on players giving it their all, together. In amateur settings, social norms and team rules tend to enforce the attendance of games and training sessions, while in professional sports settings, it's business processes backed by contracts and lawyers that define the participation of elite athletes. Irrespective of the level of professionalism, sporting teams always practise together as well as deliver (play a competitive match). Practising together is something that collaborative teams in organisations rarely do.

Another important norm regarding sporting teams is that, when they practise, they do so under the auspices of a coach who acts like a facilitator, helping the group stay on task and on time while pushing them to perform at their best. Competition schedules also motivate members to maintain a regular rhythm of collaboration, consolidating and reinforcing their shared capability. Scoreboards, rankings and the diagramming of tactics and 'plays' further contribute to the externalisation of a team's shared understanding.

So if you're looking for collaboration inspiration, sports teams have plenty to offer. When it comes to collaboration within or across our own organisations, you would do well to take a leaf out of their playbooks. At the very least, they embody how groups of people come together to perform at their best.

However, the cultures of most organisations don't value explicit support for collaboration capability, so you may face an uphill battle. As I argued earlier, it's simply assumed that a group's ability to collaborate is dependent on the capabilities of the individuals within it, not on the group's collective ability. Every group needs to build its capability by working together, which takes time, yet an allowance for this is not often made.

But you can fast-track the necessary changes. The use of specific methods to support a group of people to work better, faster and more reliably is what we call collaboration design, which is the focus of the next chapter.

CHAPTER 5

Collaboration Design

At Collabforge, we've come to understand that 'doing things by design' leads to a better outcome, and our introduction of the concept of *collaboration design* is based on this rationale. Over the course of hundreds of projects, time and time again, we've found that consciously shaping key aspects of collaboration gets a better result than leaving things to chance.

But what does adding the notion of 'design' to a word like 'collaboration' really imply? It might sound to some like an attempt to dress up an old term in new clothes, but in actual fact it draws on the growing practice of what's known as *design thinking*. Design thinking puts the participant, end user, customer, client or community (whomever benefits from the design) at the centre of your thinking, so that you can develop a deep appreciation for, and understanding of, their perspective – in a word, empathy.

Empathy, Prototyping and Setting

Developing empathy for those whom your collaboration will benefit is easier said than done. It's rarely straightforward to get them in the same room with you, and sometimes it's flat-out impossible. In fact, most Collabforge projects begin with a gathering of people with lots of capabilities, ideas, experience and inspiration, but no end users – that is, those for whom we are seeking to develop our 'solution'. This is normal practice, especially when working with government. Public servants are just that: servants to a public that has given them the social licence to collaborate in their interests. But this doesn't get them off the hook. It's still extremely important to understand the perspectives, perceptions and interests – known or unknown – of this 'public', in order to get collaboration right.

Empathy modelling is a design-thinking method that's especially valuable in addressing this aspect of collaboration design. It helps us model the perspectives of others who aren't physically present. This is particularly important when we need to design collaborative processes for people whom we may not be able to access directly, and it's often the difference between success and failure.

Some great tools are available for cultivating your understanding of others, even if you're not able to have those people physically present. I'll cover these tools in Chapter 10, which deals with the fourth stage of our process, resolving tension.

A second key aspect of design thinking is *prototyping*. Having developed a theoretical understanding of your collaboration participants and beneficiaries through empathy modelling, you can test your assumptions using a prototype. It might be a smaller, lighter version of a collaboration process you intend to use with a larger group. Or it may simply involve taking a participant through your plans and ideas, then asking for feedback before you commit to finalising them. This is an extremely effective means of soliciting crucial information for your initiative: what is most important to those with whom we wish to collaborate.

Recently, as part of embarking on a national collaboration project that was focused on climate change and carbon emissions, Collabforge helped design and run a series of workshops delivered in all of Australia's capital cities.

The twin outcomes for these workshops were to spread awareness of the project while gathering important information for an upcoming summit. Well, a key finding of the first workshop was that we'd invited the wrong participants! We'd aimed too high in appealing to more-senior leaders, who we discovered weren't able to provide the ground-level policy and program information our project needed at that stage. Fortunately, our prototype gave us the opportunity to learn and course-correct before we sent out invitations for the many other workshops we'd planned.

Prototyping can also help you quickly confirm the shared understanding and vision within a collaboration group by making concepts more tangible – if a picture says a thousand words, then a prototype shows a thousand pictures. Further, prototyping short-cuts the tendency that collaborative groups have to put off the act of creation. It almost never feels like you have enough understanding or are quite ready yet to build something as a group, whatever that something may be. But the sooner you try, the sooner you start learning through experimentation.

Prototyping can also help you understand the appropriateness of the collaboration design for your broader setting. We'll revisit the notion of collaborative *settings* throughout this book, but in simple terms, this refers to the different social contexts within which collaboration takes place. For instance, you might find yourself collaborating at work, or with your family or community, or in an emergency volunteer situation. All of these examples have different implications for collaboration design. The levels of formality versus informality, urgency versus longer-term interests, existing institutional structures versus a lack thereof – all can prompt some collaboration designs to work better than others.

These different settings and their potential variations, and how this impacts collaboration, means there is no one right answer – just the best one that you and your group can come up with at the time.

As a result, one of the highest-value design-thinking exercises you can do with your group is to have early, frank discussions about how you all understand collaboration and what it means for your specific setting, interests and objectives. And creating a prototype with your group as part of these early conversations can really kick things into gear. Cocreating a prototype needn't be complicated or difficult, either. I cover techniques for ensuring that prototyping is a fast, easy and effective part of your efforts in Chapter 9 and Chapter 11.

Bringing together holistic and empathic thinking, prototyping, experimentation and learning is what great collaboration design should do. When your participants develop a shared understanding and empathic perspectives of one another, a communal vision emerges that can be refined through discussion, externalisation and prototyping. This cycle enables your group to continuously learn how to deliver better outcomes to those within your collaborative setting.

Collaborating Consciously

Conscious collaboration is the first step of your collaboration design journey. Being actively aware of the methods and tools you'll use for collaboration dramatically increases the likelihood that they'll be a good fit for your interests and setting. However, reflecting on your collaboration design *while* you're collaborating is perhaps one of the more challenging aspects of the process.

Remaining aware of collaboration design during collaboration itself is difficult because it requires you to maintain a focus on the contributions that you and others are making, while at the same time considering how the entire process could be improved. Improvement might mean stepping back and letting others contribute or lead, or picking up a task that someone else is finding difficult, or rallying your energy to lift the spirits of those around you. You might feel that you should change activities or try a new software tool. You might need to change something about the environment or the people in the room.

As you can see, there are many things you need to keep in mind when trying to improve collaboration outcomes while simultaneously making a quality contribution yourself!

To complicate matters further, becoming conscious of the collaboration as a group, rather than as an individual, isn't always desirable. It can really disrupt your group's flow; it can make the participants self-conscious and steer their minds away from the objective of cocreation. I recommend allowing time for reflection before and after key collaborative activities and project phases, and preferably to pre-plan this. Chapter 10, on resolving tensions, details methods for improving your conscious collaboration as a group in order to also improve your shared capabilities.

Inspiring Participation

Even the best collaboration design, one that successfully balances people, process and tools, and which is developed using a design-thinking approach, requires participants who are interested enough to collaborate. Moving people from feeling comfortable to feeling inspired is a key difference-maker: the more inspired participants are, the more naturally a sense of shared ownership will arise and the more likely these people will be to prioritise the time, energy and resources needed to give it their best.

What you really need this inspiration to do is drive the social proof of participation, when one person's valuing of the collaboration is picked up by others. However, this chain reaction of interest leading to inspiration and then to social proof itself requires a catalyst, a ground zero. This role of catalyst typically falls either in part or in whole to the collaboration designer, you doing your best to embody all of the collaborative behaviours you expect from your participants – Tool 31: An Activity Catalyst, is dedicated to this. You'll almost certainly be a participant as well, and if you feel that you aren't, you should be suspicious.

I've never seen a genuine separation work very well. The collaboration designer needs to cultivate and maintain a living, empathic relationship with the others involved, and participation is simply the best way of doing this. This isn't to say that you need to be a subject-matter expert, or that your role won't evolve, with you stepping back or ultimately out of the collaboration after it's established (a very common dynamic in Collabforge projects). However, until this happens, should it be relevant to your context, do your best to maintain an active and participatory role.

The triggering of social proof for participation, in conjunction with a great collaboration design, has extraordinary potential. This is because collaboration has the ability to scale all the way up to a social movement, when large groups of people become infected by social proof and get swept up in contributing to an inspiring shared vision. Social movements represent some of the largest and most impactful collaborations the world has seen. Capitalism, communism, environmentalism, and all the major religions and scientific pursuits fall into this category. They all started with a small collaboration among a handful of individuals that eventually scaled up dramatically. So don't underestimate the potential of getting your collaboration design right.

Technological Potential

Technology is making collaboration more potent than it has ever been before. There's an ever-growing set of tools making it easier and easier to communicate and collaborate across time and space, while involving ever-larger numbers of participants. This, in combination with increasing rates of internet penetration within our local communities as well as across our continents, means there's a growing infrastructure for global collaboration. And while cultural and sociopolitical challenges are always present, nonetheless we are living in a world where it has never been easier for small groups to mobilise huge numbers of people with the right technology and methods.

In fact, from what I've seen over the past decade in my work, I anticipate a future where the tools and methods for large-scale collaboration and movement-making will be understood so well and so broadly that they'll be taken for granted (like project management). This will make strategic collaboration design a viable alternative to other tools, such as government policy, regulation, even specific elements of government itself. We're still some way from this future, but its reality is approaching.

A Common View of Collaboration

At the heart of the concept of collaboration design that I've just presented lies a very simple vision: cultivating a common view of collaboration. This shared understanding helps bring about a much greater degree of collaborative potential across society in general, as well as informing your very own project, right here and now. To be clear, this doesn't mean that we all need to hold the same view. Rather, we need reference points for what such a view might be. This lets us better argue for and against our own individual positions and build them out through research and application. This, of course, is the story of every great human endeavour, and what could be more worthwhile than creating the methods we need to work and live better together.

Taking a cue from the great collaboration that is the scientific method, I believe that a common view of collaboration should be underpinned by the creation of theories and methods that can be tested, improved and built upon, empirically. Some practitioners I've spoken to find this approach unappealing. They feel it hardens aspects of collaboration that they're used to addressing intuitively, or they claim that effective universal collaboration methods are simply not possible. But I don't agree that this is the case. I think we can build these capabilities through experimentation, at the same time maintaining, if not bolstering, the sensitivity, empathy and flexibility that these practitioners have cultivated.

The next chapter provides the key elements of what I've called *a general theory of collaboration* – three principles that have held up over time, informing the design of hundreds of collaborations with government organisations. These three principles should help you better understand and apply the Collabforge method outlined in Part II, which uses this general theory as its basis. However, I also hope that by sharing this theory, the development of ever-better methods of collaboration design will be inspired and accelerated. So you can consider this an invitation to challenge, expand or adapt these ideas in ways that support your own collaboration needs and world view.

CHAPTER 6

The Three Principles of Collaboration

Shared ideas, shared process and shared capability, the three principles of collaboration I describe here, are at their simplest a way of understanding how collaboration works in all situations, at all scales, in all cultures – a general theory of collaboration, if you will. These ideas originated in my own PhD but have evolved throughout the hundreds of collaboration projects I've conducted at Collabforge with my dedicated and brilliant colleagues and our wonderful clients.

The three principles, from which arise the six-stage Collabforge method and its 36 tools, enable us to deliver reliably great collaboration for many government agencies, large organisations and innovating teams.

First Principle - Shared Ideas

Collaboration creates shared ideas that generate feedback when externalised.

All collaborative activities, outputs and outcomes start as ideas. These ideas begin their lives in the minds of individuals, but as they're communicated and shared, they spread to the minds of others. As collaboration continues, these shared ideas become increasingly aligned and transformed by their interactions with one another, in the process spawning new ideas. Participants externalise these newly cocreated ideas into the environment, often via some form of media. This accelerates the whole process by creating feedback, while increasing the participants' collective memory, their capacity to address complexity, and their ability to manipulate and share the ideas. As this happens, these shared ideas become tangible collaborative outputs that impact the people around the participants – the final outcome of a collaboration.

Shared ideas can therefore be said to be the essence, if not the heart, of collaboration. They are the snowy peaks of the mountains from which all other collaborative outcomes flow. This is why the Collabforge method places such great importance on cultivating a shared understanding early on. This can be the first collaborative outcome that a group produces, helping to validate the premise for collaboration while creating a foundation for any and all new ideas that follow.

This moment of translation, when the ideas held in the minds of collaboration participants are externalised to become real-world outputs and actions, is a critical point in the collaboration process. It creates a feedback loop, driving the refinement and improvement of both the ideas and the outputs – the ideas can be influenced by the impact of their tangible manifestation, which in turn can influence subsequent manifestations. How well this feedback process works is directly affected by the type of medium the ideas are externalised into, as well as the types of activities that drive the externalisation.

A group focused on an ecosystem of people, organisations and government policy for an industry sector will likely arrive at different conclusions if, instead of basic conversation, they're supported by a digital tool that allows them to collaboratively build a network visualisation of this ecosystem in real time. Alternatively, collaborating musicians may get a better result by simply jamming, as opposed to trying to first sketch out their musical inspirations and ideas on a whiteboard. Different approaches to creating feedback, as ideas are externalised, will get better or worse results for different people in different situations.

Determining the right approach, activities and media for your participants, their setting and interests, is the objective of collaboration design. The principle of shared ideas is the premise of this rationale, and the foundation of the Collabforge method.

One of Collabforge's first projects, FutureMelbourne, illustrated the successful application of this principle. The goal of this project was to 're-engineer' the City of Melbourne's 10-year strategic planning process for better collaboration. This had become a priority because it had been recognised that having a few people lock themselves away in a room filled with butcher's paper and sticky notes didn't always produce the ideal outcome, one aligned with the interests of all involved. Genuine collaboration was seen as a key strategy for creating a better outcome because it could help ensure that all stakeholders have a meaningful say. If the city's institutions, businesses and taxpayers could meaningfully contribute to the strategic plan, then their needs and interests would be more authentically addressed. Equally as important, they would feel a sense of shared ownership of the final output and have a vested interest in its realisation. This outcome was especially valuable because the 10-year strategic plan is the highest-level planning framework the city has – all other plans and strategies align below it – and its success depends on the degree to which the community supports it.

Over the course of a year or so, Collabforge took a holistic approach to developing and delivering a collaboration design that resulted in 'the city plan that anyone can edit' (this was our tagline, with an explicit nod to Wikipedia). We were able to engage with and involve nearly 20,000 people around the world. I will speak more about how FutureMelbourne worked in later sections of this book, but the point I want to make here is that a key innovation of this project was the creation of an online wiki platform to support the collaborative drafting of the 10-year plan. It provided the means for the genuine involvement of stakeholders in the drafting process, facilitating the externalisation of their ideas directly into the draft city plan.

This meant that people didn't have to wait their turn in town hall meetings to make their point; they could log on then and there and literally write their ideas into the plan itself. And because the city's planners were using the same platform to write the plan, they could quickly address and incorporate the public contributions, while letting the contributors know how they had done this. This delivered the multiple benefits of rapid moderation, facilitation and editorial functions, as well as highly collaborative public engagement.

As the contributions came in from formal stakeholders and the public, the FutureMelbourne team realised they were receiving a steady stream of collaborative inputs in the right format – that is, actual content for the plan, as opposed to critical commentary about it. This closed the feedback loop, influencing the ideas of the planners as they refined the plan's content, while helping them better understand the public's interests; for example, sustainability and carbon neutrality. As well as directly editing the plan, participants could also comment on or edit other people's work, including that of the city planners, and access a full revision history of every section.

The final plan that was signed off by Melbourne's mayor and councillors was a genuine representation of all the ideas and interactions that had taken place prior to its finalisation – an outcome that can't often be claimed for government public consultations. The plan went on to win industry awards for both its process and content.

While strategy and planning collaborations lend themselves particularly well to illustrating the relationship between shared ideas and their externalisation, you will see the feedback loop this creates in all collaborations once you start looking. However, there's still much to understand about how this happens in different situations and the support processes involved – which brings us to the second principle of collaboration.

Second Principle - Shared Process

Collaboration requires participation in a common set of processes.

It should be self-evident that, for collaboration to work, participants must engage in a common, shared process. What's less evident is exactly what this process is. During my doctoral research, I found that three different but interrelated processes – cocreation, cooperation and coordination – together contribute to making collaboration work (see Figure 3).

Figure 3. The 3Cs of Collaboration: Cocreation, Cooperation and Coordination

As you move up from coordination through cooperation to cocreation, you can address more complexity with regard to ideas and what can be externalised. And because these three processes are interrelated, each requires its predecessor as a foundation for the next. So if you're going to cooperate, you'll need a foundation of coordination. Similarly, cocreation requires both cooperation and coordination.

While these three terms will be familiar to you, I'm going to suggest more-specific definitions than what you might find in a dictionary, geared towards describing the generation of collaborative outcomes.

COORDINATION

Coordination looks the least like what you would recognise as collaboration – at least, collaboration as typified by workshop-type interactions. Coordination happens when ideas, things and/or people are drawn together into a space that foregrounds a pattern or relationship. This pattern or relationship allows those involved to act (knowingly or unknowingly) with new-found intelligence and insight.

A classic example of coordination is how a great conference gathers together diverse people in a structured environment to bring about *designed serendipity*. As an attendee, you might find yourself apparently randomly chatting with the person seated next to you, marvelling at what a great connection you've just made. Another example is how a well-designed park can encourage the right types of activities in specific areas – picnics, ball games, dogs running off-leash, and so on – so that they don't disturb each other.

Search engines such as Google also deliver coordination outcomes through their lists of search results. Digital assets are drawn together in an ordered list (a pattern), allowing you to quickly assess the results. In fact, a big part of assessing the merits of your search results is the degree to which the individual results relate to one another – the more they do, the more successful your search term. This is a common feature of coordination: the pattern that emerges seems to suggest an actual relationship between the individual elements that have been brought together, even though there may be none other than the pattern.

COOPERATION

Cooperation requires a foundation of coordination in order to create the opportunity for participants to make contributions to a shared process. At a minimum, the participants must be well enough coordinated regarding their culture, language and norms to understand and value a given cooperative process. They'll also likely need to be coordinated within space and time to participate. And like coordination, cooperation doesn't rely on participants explicitly interacting with one another. Instead, they can interact via a process that links their contributions together.

Surveys are a simple example. Consider a survey of 1000 people on any given topic. The participants contribute without interacting with one another, while the aggregation of their responses and the compilation of a result links their individual contributions into a greater whole. This greater whole delivers value by providing insight into what the participants think about a given issue. Cooperation is a go-to method for engaging people because of its scalability – it's far more efficient to run a survey with 1000 participants than it is to have separate conversations with each of them.

Innovations in cooperative processes were evident throughout the Industrial Revolution; for example, automobile factory lines where workers progressively added individual elements until a fully functioning car had been built. Company reporting lines and organisational charts also follow the core principles of cooperation. Business processes aggregate the contributions made by individuals and teams, with the eventual outcome being the delivery of products or services, and, hopefully, profits.

A trait of cooperative processes is that the contributions are typically very transactional. They require little to no negotiation and can be clearly defined: a price is displayed on a product in a supermarket, you pay that price at the cash register, and the product is now yours and the money is the supermarket's. Another key trait is that one contribution doesn't influence or change another. Once a vote is cast in a ballot box, for example, it won't change despite someone else voting for a different candidate.

COCREATION

Cocreation, the heart of collaboration, is quite different to cooperation and coordination. One person's contribution almost always influences the contributions that follow, and may even affect those that came before. Whether in conversation, co-authoring a document, or drawing something on a whiteboard with someone else, when you're genuinely creating with another person, it's pretty much the point that your input will influence someone else's.

A person influencing others through their participation is exactly why cocreation is such a powerful mode of engagement. For example, cocreating a strategy with those who will be subjected to it can actually do a lot of the work of the strategy itself, pushing the authors to think through the strategy's implications as they draft it. Participating in a creative process also tends to shift people's perspectives from being critical – 'What is this thing I'm looking at and what do and don't I like about it?' – to being constructive – 'How can I improve this thing and its chances of success as I work on it?' Generating shared ownership through cocreation is gold when it comes to developing not just strategies but products, services, policies, programs and processes – anything that can significantly determine the experiences of others.

Returning to the FutureMelbourne example, the key interest of Collabforge was to establish cocreation opportunities for the wider community, with a supportive culture, process and tool set. We wanted stakeholders and the public to be less critical and more constructive in their attitudes towards the city plan, and we especially wanted them to develop a sense of shared ownership of it through genuine participation in its creation. The idea was that this would contribute towards the most important outcome of all – ultimately, widespread support and participation in the plan's implementation. But at the outset of this project, it wasn't immediately clear just how we would do all this.

To understand where the opportunities for this broader cocreation might lie, we first mapped the existing 10-year planning process, identifying where cocreation, cooperation and coordination would happen if we changed nothing. We then considered what changes to the planning process might benefit the outcome, while also thinking about how this would impact its more formal aspects. From this arose a blueprint for how the collaboration would unfold over the coming months: what kind of collaborative processes would be involved, how they would be staged out, who would participate, and when.

One thing that immediately stood out from this mapping was that the internal planning team would handle and drive the majority of the planning cocreation. They held the greatest knowledge of Melbourne's overall planning priorities, and had been resourced to manage and ultimately deliver the 10-year plan as a document to council. This team was going to be ground zero for a collaboration that we wanted to scale up significantly beyond them, so it was important to involve them in developing the collaboration design to make sure they felt comfortable involving others at later stages.

From a cooperation perspective, we recognised that the key players would be the mayor, councillors and the city's senior executives, as well as a steering committee that had been set up to oversee the process. The involvement of these participants would be fairly transactional in nature – we'd provide them with project updates and reports, to which they'd react, getting back to us with their advice and decisions. This understanding meant that we could involve them in the right way and at the right time, appropriate to the process of cooperation, as opposed to cocreation or coordination.

By far the largest group involved were those who fell into the category of coordination. As with all major planning initiatives, millions of people could be affected over time, and it was essential to keep them informed of the impacts. We also wanted to make sure that as many people as possible were kept aware of the opportunities to participate.

As this example illustrates, *the* 3*Cs* of cocreation, cooperation and coordination provide a means of categorising and catering to your stakeholders and participants. In fact, Tool 8: Participant Mapping for the Core, Community and Crowd, applies the 3Cs to stakeholder mapping. Beyond such mapping, they can also serve as the basis for understanding what activities can be used to deliver different outcomes, and what tools and technologies will be needed to support those activities.

Throughout the rest of this book, the principle of shared process, and the 3Cs that anchor it, will serve as the foundation for understanding how collaboration works. So keep in mind that, any time these three terms are used, it will be in reference to the definitions provided above.

Third Principle – Shared Capability

The capability to resolve tension and create shared value is distributed. As participants externalise their ideas and take various actions in the real world, they build a collaborative capability that is unique to their specific personalities, needs, interests and experiences. What is important about this capability, and the third principle of collaboration, is that it's *shared* between the participants. The ability of the partakers to collaborate depends on the understandings, methods, processes and techniques that are held between them, more so than those held by any one individual.

The individual engaged in collaboration doesn't work in isolation – whatever they do affects the other people involved. Further, how well they do what they do is a direct input to how well the group works as a whole. It doesn't matter how much collaborative experience or ability any one participant has if this doesn't translate into a shared practice with the other members. With no *shared* capability, the group will just be a bunch of individuals working by themselves.

The challenging implication of shared capability is that the members of every new group, irrespective of how much collaborative experience is held by any individual, will need to build a shared practice together. This means that when a collaboration gets going, the participants are typically working at their lowest capability. They may get results early on, but rarely will it represent their best work as a group. Participants need to negotiate interpersonal styles, interests and understandings, as well as specific approaches, processes and tools, in order to bring their best to the actual subject matter of the collaboration.

This early phase can be challenged by yet another dynamic. The tensions that arise naturally as part of collaboration can take a great many forms, ranging from confusion and a lack of understanding, through to differences in opinion or ways of working. When collaborative capability is low, any tension can slow down and even stop collaboration in its tracks.

The sooner participants begin to gain experience in resolving tension together, ideally in a de-risked, even playful context, the more likely it is that they'll overcome these early hurdles and have the skills needed when it really counts. Because of its importance, the fourth stage of collaboration (see Chapter 10) is dedicated entirely to constructively recognising, raising and resolving tensions, which will ultimately determine the quality of the collaboration's outcomes.

A critical shift when thinking about tension in the context of collaboration is to recognise that tension, in and of itself, is not a bad thing. It's not an indication that the group is unaligned, nor that something is going wrong. It is certainly *not* something to be avoided. Rather, albeit perhaps counterintuitively, directly and successfully engaging with and resolving tension is precisely where collaboration derives its value – as I discussed in Chapter 4. This is because the primary purpose of collaboration is to transform the ideas held by individuals into new ideas shared by a group. This transformation represents a move from a state of dissonance, where ideas just don't quite fit together or feel right, to one of consonance, where the ideas seem to click into place – often a breakthrough or 'Ah-ha!' moment. When a new shared representation is created, it brings the group into a greater degree of alignment and collective focus. Typically, the greater the tension that's resolved, the greater the value delivered through collaboration.

Returning again to the FutureMelbourne example, the Collabforge approach of involving the core planning team in the codesign of the collaboration helped to set up the necessary capability early and quickly. This naturally spurred many conversations about collaboration: its applications, tools, benefits and risks. And as this happened, we made time to reflect on our own experiences and practices as a team, which had the effect of accelerating the development of our own group capability.

Our core group also needed to build capability with the executive steering committee. That committee had the power to block anything we wanted to do – it was their responsibility to fully understand what we were proposing, and only then to sign off on it. The FutureMelbourne project lead and manager of strategic planning for the city was actually a member of both groups. This meant that he was able to translate for the steering committee some of the core group's methods and even capability in a substantive and consistent way, helping them to feel comfortable with our approach, despite how different it was from their normal way of working and the perceived riskiness of involving the community in the plan's cocreation.

These efforts proved essential when we sought the committee's approval to grant the general public access to the online collaboration platform. This decision – to provide open access to anyone in the world so that they could add, edit or delete plan content – was naturally seen as fraught. We'd successfully used the platform for internal collaboration and for work with key stakeholders, but making it accessible to the broader public was a different matter. When one councillor said, 'So, as I understand it, if we do this, anyone can come along and upload porn to the site?', I thought for sure that our radical approach to collaboration would end then and there. However, the shared capability we'd built with the committee helped convey to the councillors not only the strength of our strategic approach, but also how we were mitigating risks (through a detailed monitoring, moderation and escalation plan). They felt comfortable enough to give it a try – and, of course, they recognised the goodwill that could be established with the community by offering such a potent way to engage.

The ultimate outcome of FutureMelbourne was an award-winning plan that has stood the test of time – and politics. A decade and several mayors and councils later, the plan is still in place, with only relatively minor updates and changes having occurred. Central to this success was the resolution of dissonance not only within the core team, but also among the steering committee, stakeholders and the public. A collaboration design based on the principles of shared ideas, process and capability was crucial for a strategic, holistic and well-executed approach.

Part II

The Collabforge Method

Using This Method

The method presented in the following chapters is structured according to six stages: decide, convene, cocreate, resolve, maintain and grow. Together, they provide a way of understanding and pursuing the grand arc of collaboration. A chapter is dedicated to each of these stages, each of them acting as a high-level signpost that will cue you to develop your design as you navigate your way along the journey of collaboration.

Keep in mind as you progress, however, that these stages don't work like the stages in a recipe. Simply following them to the letter won't necessarily result in a perfectly baked cake. Rather, they function more like stairs: you go up and down as needed – sometimes, you might only get halfway up before turning around and coming back down. This is because when you collaborate, you often need to revisit earlier stages as you move ahead to new ones. For example, a workshop during stage three (cocreation) might establish that you need to involve new participants. In this case, you'd need to move back down to the second stage (convening a collaboration) in order to onboard those people.

Each stage also acts as a container of sorts for some of the 36 tools that I've included in this book. These tools are simple, practical activities that the team at Collabforge has used over many years to deliver great collaboration results. Some of them are simple thinking activities, prompting you to give due consideration to aspects you may not have otherwise contemplated. But many of them involve step-by-step instructions to be carried out – sometimes by you alone, sometimes with your collaborative peers – which have been designed to create a specific output or outcome. You will get the most out of these tools if you follow their steps, even if just for a hypothetical scenario, as this will more fully activate the part of your mind that's used for simulating collaboration. In fact, one of the key skills needed for collaboration design is the ability to play out a range of scenarios conceptually, to get a feel for how they might work.

The tools and the methodology have been developed with reference to the three principles discussed in Chapter 6. While you'll probably feel more confident collaborating and get better results if you fully understand these principles, the method is nonetheless designed to work independently from them. So don't worry if you're still feeling a little foggy on that front. Read on, and I'll revisit the principles where required.

CHOOSING A SCENARIO

As you work your way through Part II, try to have in mind an existing or potential collaboration that you can apply the method to. That way, you'll get the most out of learning this approach.

To help you choose a collaborative scenario, I'd ask you to pause and think about the projects or initiatives you're currently involved in or actively planning, as well as the ones you're considering for the future. Specifically, consider which of these would either benefit from collaboration or clearly require it. Try to identify three options.

Now pick one of these three, whichever one feels the most exciting, important or impactful. It's OK if it's a half-baked idea – some of the best collaborations start with very modest concepts that evolve as the participants make their contributions.

From here on out, when working through a tool, please apply it to the scenario you've selected. If for some reason the scenario doesn't feel like a good fit, or if you want to try out a tool on a different scenario, that's fine – feel free to switch. The important thing is that you apply the tools to a specific situation. As I mentioned earlier, cultivating your ability to mentally simulate collaborative interactions is an essential part of building your collaboration design capability.

A WORK IN PROGRESS

A final point before we move on: I'd encourage you to treat this method as a work in progress. Humanity is barely on the threshold of a rich understanding of collaboration. I expect this knowledge to grow considerably in the coming years. So as you follow the Collabforge method and learn for yourself the art of great collaboration design, I hope you'll be inspired to build on this starting point by sharing any insights with me. In the conclusion to this book, I've provided the means to get in touch, should you want to dive deeper and contribute to the improvement of this and other methods. Me and the rest of the team here at Collabforge are eager to connect with kindred spirits, inspired by the promise and potential of better collaboration design.

CHAPTER 7

Decide

Making a *conscious* decision to collaborate is the first stage of great collaboration. It forces you to weigh up the expected costs and benefits involved. In essence, you'll develop a hypothesis about the potential for collaboration in your context: how it might work, who will be involved, according to what premise, and so on. And as science has taught us, a hypothesis can be a very powerful thing: once you have one, you can test it, learn from the results, and improve it.

To help you reach a quality decision, as well as inform a hypothesis, this chapter presents five tools. They'll allow you to probe the different dimensions of a collaboration in order to make a holistic assessment of its risks and opportunities, as well as its strengths and weaknesses. The first two tools are focused more on your individual interests, to make sure they're being served first and foremost. The remaining tools shift to an external orientation so that you can assess the interests and capabilities of your prospective co-collaborators, and the resources and conditions present in the environment that will either support or constrain your collaboration.

A Note on the Drivers of Collaboration

Before we jump into how to develop and test a hypothesis for collaboration, let's first reflect on what drives the more-instinctual approach to collaboration that most people tend to take. Our instincts for collaboration can be powerful, driving us into certain circumstances before we've even consciously chosen them. The method outlined in this book provides you with the tools to explicitly leverage these less-conscious aspects of decision-making in your collaboration design.

FUN

There's little so pleasurable as a team win. Sharing our work and experiences with others is perhaps one of the more common human interests. It's one of the main reasons why collaborating can make work more enjoyable and time seem to pass more quickly. We are social creatures who like spending time with our friends: those who play together stay together ... birds of a feather flock together ... you get the picture.

What's important to remember here is not just that we often collaborate with others for fun and comfort, but that we frequently use this as the basis for assessing collaborative opportunities. There's nothing wrong with this – unless, that is, it blinds us to other opportunities. We can all too easily fall into the trap of only working with those whom we usually work with, which ignores the possibilities that working with new people brings: new ideas, connections, resources, experiences. So try to ensure, when considering a collaborative opportunity, that you aren't blinded by the potential for fun or comfort.

On the other hand, don't stop considering the prospects for fun and the enjoyment of relationships. If you can't spot any, it may be a signal that you won't be able to bring your best to the situation. Similarly, when communicating a collaboration opportunity to others, make sure you highlight the potential for fun that you feel it offers. Fun is a powerful motivator!

POTENTIAL

Increasing the potential of the individual is possibly our most common rationale for taking a collaborative approach. Being exposed to the experiences, expertise, diversity and resources of others raises new possibilities that would otherwise not have existed. Indeed, when faced with a complex challenge, recognising that you may not have all the answers is often your first instinctive cue to collaborate.

The promise of increased potential should be tempered by recognition of the fact that not all tasks lend themselves to collaboration. This is largely due to how the benefits of bringing collaborative potential to a challenge or opportunity aren't always needed. Some topics ultimately aren't complex enough to warrant the time and energy that collaboration requires, and instead of getting better results, participants just get fatigued or frustrated. However, when a challenge truly is complex – that is, it has many interdependent stakeholders and elements, while needing an outcome that requires a decent amount of creativity – it's likely that the only way to get a great result is to bring more folks into the mix.

That said, you shouldn't assume that you'll automatically increase your collaborative potential simply by getting more people into a room and providing strong facilitation. You still need an effective collaboration design, which is the premise of the Collabforge method.

SUPPORT

There's perhaps no greater driver of success in collaboration than shared ownership. This approach works because, as I mentioned in the introduction to this book, it's a very rare person who wants to see their own creation fail. We tend to care more about, and put more energy into, the things we feel we own, or have played a part in creating. Whether it's a business, a hobby, a work of art, a machine, a relationship or a child, our creations tend to ignite our passions and energies above all other activities.

Therefore, as a collective creative process, collaboration should cultivate a sense of shared ownership among its participants. By doing so, it progressively transforms each participant from an outsider with a critical eye, into a member of the family who does everything they can to fuel the success of *their* initiative. Shared ownership generates more support, inspiration and awareness when it comes to what you're trying to achieve – participants will be ready to go to bat for each other and the shared vision.

Putting on our strategic hats, this in fact means that drawing a decision-maker into a collaboration can be a very clever way of gaining their support and understanding. Imagine your boss increasing your funding and championing your cause because they see themselves as a co-owner of your idea after having helped you shape or reshape it.

Seeing collaboration as a strategic approach to gaining the support you need, whatever this means in your context, is one of the less common but more sophisticated drivers of collaboration.

Tool 1: Your Value Proposition for Collaboration

As its title suggests, this tool helps inform your for/against decision by establishing *your* value proposition for a collaboration; that is to say, what's in it for you personally, as opposed to anyone else, or an organisation you may be working for.

With your actual/hypothetical collaboration in mind, carefully consider each of the following questions and choose the most relevant answer. This shouldn't take you more than five minutes.

STEP 1: CAN YOU DO IT BY YOURSELF?

If you feel that the answer to this question might be 'No', think about why this is the case, and what would be the greatest benefits of collaboration.

On the other hand, if the answer feels like a 'Yes', consider whether the outcome could be improved by involving others, and if so, what these benefits might be.

Now make your choice.

1 Yes
2 Maybe
3 No

STEP 2: ARE YOUR OWN INTERESTS COMPELLING, VALUABLE OR ENERGISING?

Don't answer this question on behalf of an organisation or anyone else, like your boss. Contemplate what's in it for you personally. How much does the scenario, outcome or its impact excite you?

1 Low
2 Medium
3 High

STEP 3: HOW MUCH COMPLEXITY IS INVOLVED, AND HOW MUCH CREATIVITY OR DIVERSITY OF PERSPECTIVES IS REQUIRED?

Are you considering collaboration to address complexity, or can the problem be broken down into incrementally solvable elements? If the latter, is there a high level of interdependence between these elements, or between the interests of those involved (stakeholders, participants, beneficiaries and so on)? What levels of creativity will be required to produce great outcomes? Make a selection after considering all of these factors.

1 Low
2 Medium
3 High

STEP 4: DETERMINE YOUR SCORE

Add up the numbers that correspond to the answers you selected for each question and divide the total by 3. For example, if you selected

'Yes' for step 1, 'High' for step 2 and 'High' for step 3, then your score would be 7 / 3 = 2.3.

If you scored a 3, assume that you must collaborate. It's a strong indication that collaboration is necessary for you to deliver a compelling and impactful outcome. A score of 3 also suggests that the initiative itself represents high value in regard to your own personal interests, that it might well be a source of inspiration and energy. This is the kind of collaborative project that can make a big difference to your career, perhaps your life.

If you landed anywhere in the 2 range, then collaboration is worth considering, but perhaps with less cocreation. For example, if you feel you can't complete the project yourself, but that while the subject matter isn't very complex, it's still a compelling opportunity, then you might consider a more cooperative approach. You could develop a brief for someone who has the necessary skills or expertise to deliver some or all of the work for you. This requires far less energy and effort than designing and delivering a full-blown collaboration that involves significant cocreation.

Alternatively, perhaps you feel that you can develop the solution by yourself and that the outcome is very valuable to you, but delivery will be constrained by a highly complex bureaucratic, social or political environment. In this case, collaboration could be a good support strategy, as outlined in the previous section. In this type of situation, getting the work done often isn't the same as getting the impact desired. For example, you may be fully capable of generating a particular strategy on your own, but if you don't involve other key stakeholders in its development, they may not have sufficient interest or understanding to back you in implementing whatever you draft.

If you got 2s or 3s for steps 1 and 3 but believe that the initiative ultimately isn't of great interest to you, or isn't inspiring, be very wary of any collaboration. More than anything else, collaboration requires your inspiration because of the social proof needed to get others involved. If they don't see that you're personally excited, they'll be much less likely to participate. Or if they do, it's unlikely to be for the right reasons (for example, they may agree to take part because they feel obligated to), which means that you won't get what you need to sustain the collaboration. Similarly, if you got a score in the 1 range, you should definitely consider not collaborating at all, for these same reasons.

If, after applying this tool, you're still not clear about the value proposition for collaboration for you personally, then test your ideas with a few trusted prospective participants. Sometimes the benefits of collaboration can only be fully understood through a little collaboration – you may not know what others can bring to the situation, and thus the potential for a collaboration, without digging into it a little with them.

In 2013, Collabforge worked with the City of Melbourne to help it develop a digital strategy. This turned into a very unconventional project, based on the insightful assessment by the chief information officer (CIO) of the collaboration requirements. The CIO's team acknowledged the city's need to understand how it should prepare for and support a digital future. However, the team knew there was a significantly greater understanding of what this future might look like outside of the organisation, in the wider community, than within its own walls. For one thing, Melbourne has a vibrant tech scene that can be consulted, and many of these folks are voting ratepayers. So the levels of complexity and interdependence were very high, as was the value proposition for a great outcome. Further, regarding the development of a strategy, a good deal of creativity would be involved, as there was no *right* answer – just the best one for the people involved, using the resources at hand, at that particular time. The City of Melbourne team felt they would struggle to come up with the best answer without wide and substantive community input.

While our client didn't formally take the value proposition test, recalling our discussions, I'm confident they would've scored a solid 3. In the end, we ran an *unconference*, a highly collaborative process that enables participants to create their own conference agenda and content on the day. This event brought together about 200 entrepreneurs, innovators, public servants, researchers, educators and generally interested Melbournians. Over the course of a weekend, we all shared and developed ideas, understandings and projects. This allowed the City of Melbourne to learn direct from the community what the local digital future might look like, and how to translate this into a strategic approach.

Tool 2: The Collaboration Premium

The Collaboration Premium is a straightforward-to-use tool that can help you arrive at a 'Yes' or 'No' conclusion regarding collaboration, especially within strategic organisational settings. This tool was originally presented in Morten Hansen's book *Collaboration* (2009), a guide for business executives who are considering internal collaboration as a way of gaining a strategic advantage. For the purposes of the Collabforge method, I've simplified Hansen's original approach to make it more applicable to collaboration settings beyond corporate environments.

The tool follows a simple equation:

collaboration premium = return on project –
opportunity costs – collaboration costs

The idea here is that collaboration should only be considered if the net value – the collaboration premium – is greater than the expected return, minus both the opportunity costs *and* the costs that collaboration itself will entail. In short, your collaboration premium should be a net gain, not a negative number.

STEP 1: CONSIDER YOUR EXPECTED RETURN ON COLLABORATION

As in step 2 of Tool 1, consider your personal interests regarding collaboration, but now include those of the prospective individual participants and any organisations involved. With these perspectives in mind, answer the following questions:

1. Do you expect a monetary return from the collaboration? For example, might there be new or increased sales, product or service development, investment opportunities, operational efficiencies, or other benefits that are translatable financially? What's the estimated gain?
2. Do you expect intangible returns for you, your participants or your organisation? These might be new or improved relationships, networks, knowledge, influence, ideas, opportunities, or access to physical spaces or other resources currently beyond your reach.

Now determine, on balance, whether the overall expected return on collaboration is:

1. Low
2. Medium
3. High

STEP 2: CONSIDER YOUR OPPORTUNITY COST

Your opportunity cost is what you'll be unable to do if you decide to collaborate, because collaboration takes time and energy that could be dedicated to other pursuits. Consider these questions:

1. Is there a new or existing activity, interest, project or priority that would come to the foreground if you didn't collaborate? How might you evaluate this alternative in terms of its value or interest to you?
2. Is there another less-intensive way of achieving your goal that minimises cocreation? For example, could you take a more cooperative approach, whereby others deliver

prescribed elements on your behalf? Can this be quantified in terms of time and money?

3 Will collaboration close the door on other opportunities? For example, could it create a specific situation that non-participants might see as competitive, thereby making it difficult or impossible to work with them at a later date?

Now work out if your expected opportunity cost is:

1 High
2 Medium
3 Low

STEP 3: CONSIDER THE COSTS OF COLLABORATION

Often, collaboration costs actual cash. It can also cost *in-kind* money – that is, goods or services already paid for, or paid for from another source; for example, someone's salaried time, where an organisation covers their participation period. Other costs might involve particular tools or technology, a facilitator or other expert participant, even content creation and markcting.

Now consider what cash or in-kind costs might be involved in a collaboration. What might these amount to? (A rough estimate is fine.)

Less tangible but equally important to consider are the time and energy required of all participants. How intensive will the project be? If it's likely to be draining and not-so-inspiring for those involved, consider the cost to be high. However, if the project will be energising and uplifting, this can offset the 'energy cost' of collaboration. On balance, the costs (both financial and intangible) of collaborating will be:

1 High
2 Medium
3 Low

STEP 4: CALCULATE YOUR PREMIUM

Add the numbers corresponding to your answers and divide by 3. The closer your score is to a 3, the higher your collaboration premium.

Keep in mind, though, that this tool is not meant to provide a quantitative and conclusive result so much as a means of reflecting more deeply on a given opportunity. This tool should also surface reasons both for and against collaboration that you haven't previously considered, which will be valuable inputs to your collaboration design.

A Note on the Three Levels of Collaboration

A big part of coming to a conscious decision regarding collaboration is simply thinking more deeply about what will be involved, as there are many ways in which collaboration can be done. A major constraint on how your collaboration can be designed is what I call the *level* of collaboration. At Collabforge, we've identified three levels where collaboration primarily takes place, from the perspective of the complexity being addressed, the types of people involved, and their interactions: team, representative and system (see Figure 4).

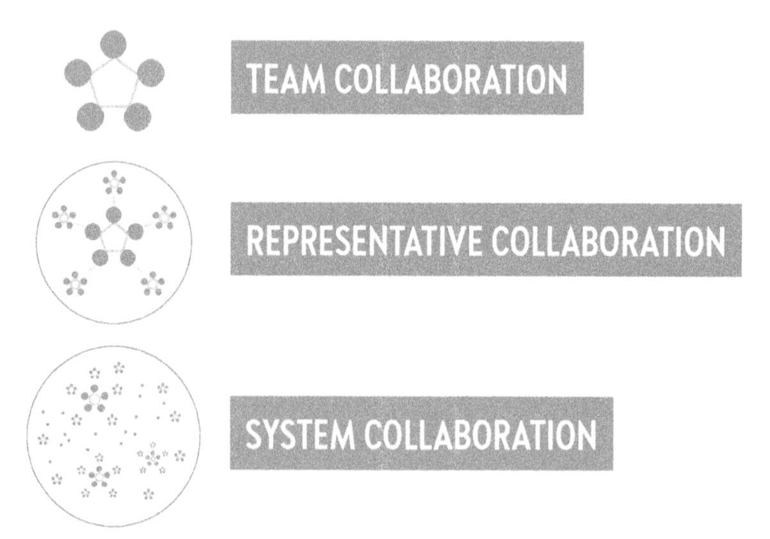

Figure 4. The Three Levels of Collaboration

None of these levels is of more significance than any other when it comes to considering whether or not you should collaborate. However, the specific level will greatly influence the intensity of the collaboration, what types of tools to use, and what other resources and support you may need. Thinking about the level of collaboration informs your decision by helping you understand the bigger picture, and what you'll need to realise your collaboration premium.

The *team* level concerns the type of collaboration that people are most familiar with. Those involved are grouped into a single team, or into two or more teams whose overall vision is more or less the same – the joint delivery of a project, product or service, for example. Members of these teams generate a substantive shared understanding and vision around a common goal, largely through cocreation. This enables the division of labour among members and interrelated teams. However, the need for ongoing cocreation and coordination to maintain alignment is ever-present, which means regular working sessions, meetings and team check-ins.

One level up is *representative*. This is where those who represent the interests of others collaborate. These representatives may be politicians advocating on behalf of their constituents, or executives advocating on behalf of stakeholders in their part of a business, or community leaders or sports team coaches. They typically do not interact in the substantive way that those engaged in team collaboration do. Nevertheless, their collaboration and even their cocreation must deliver outcomes that keep things working well for those represented.

Lastly, the *system* level involves a mix of team and representative collaboration, plus individuals who interact with both of these levels. This is where whole-of-organisation collaboration takes place, with a complex system of interactions creating unpredictable ebbs and flows of communication, activity and outcomes. Many teams are usually in play, as are representatives, processes and technologies. There are also many individuals who move freely in and out of the system, such as staff entering or exiting an organisation, or consultants and other 'externals' who attend meetings and participate in various projects.

Larger community collaborations can also exhibit system-level characteristics. For example, the not-for-profit organisation behind Wikipedia, the Wikimedia Foundation, and the website's community-coordinated management involve a great deal of representative collaboration, while individuals and teams of editors also work together to build and maintain the online encyclopedia.

For now, it's enough to reflect on what the primary level of your own collaboration will be. The higher the level, the more detailed your collaboration design should be. A higher level also typically corresponds to an increase in the time, energy and resourcing required.

At Collabforge, we often use this framework when considering the requirements of a given project. We know that delivering a collaboration design for a team comprising three sub-teams (team collaboration) is considerably easier than delivering one for an organisational strategy (representative collaboration). Both are vastly easier than delivering a collaboration design for an organisational entity (system collaboration).

Tool 3: Support for Collaboration

One of the most obvious factors at play when you're deciding whether or not to collaborate is how strongly you feel about your chances of success or failure. Understanding your level of collaboration is helpful because it can assist you in assessing the scale of the challenge. This tool goes further by breaking up that challenge into three categories: value, goodwill and resources. When all three are strong, so too are the prospects for success.

STEP 1: WHAT IS THE PERCEIVED VALUE AND URGENCY OF THE OUTCOME?

The more the outcomes of your collaboration are valued by the participants, the more likely it is that your initiative will get off the ground and maintain its momentum. Imagine what your participants will value most, should your proposed collaboration succeed. If you're having trouble with this, try making a list of your participants and considering their value propositions one at a time, starting with whom you feel is most needed for success.

Are these outcomes likely to be perceived as high-value for participants? Will they be perceived as urgent? Make a selection accordingly:

1 Low
2 Medium
3 High

STEP 2: HOW MUCH GOODWILL IS PRESENT AT THE OUTSET?

Goodwill is essential for collaboration in all settings. In organisational settings, goodwill drives trust – it's the grease that prevents collaboration from coming to a grinding halt when tensions arise. In less-formal contexts, such as at home, goodwill can be a primary driver, without which collaboration will likely not be possible.

Do you feel that the levels of goodwill among the individuals and organisations involved will be strong? Are there any individuals who might spark ill will due to their personalities, histories, biases, or how they may be perceived by others? Is there anyone who might have the opposite effect, sparking goodwill simply by their presence?

Estimate the level of goodwill:

1 Low
2 Medium
3 High

STEP 3: WHAT RESOURCES ARE PRESENT AT THE OUTSET?

Depending on your collaborative venture, some combination of money, human resources and skills will be needed. Will your participants value the outcome enough to contribute these? What about time and energy, which are in short supply for most people? And if the participants can't contribute as fully as you'd like, might they be motivated to help get any missing resources?

Choose the level of resourcing you'll have from the start of the collaboration:

1 Low
2 Medium
3 High

STEP 4: CALCULATE THE LEVEL OF YOUR COLLABORATIVE SUPPORT

Add up the numbers corresponding to your answers and divide the total by 3. The closer your score is to a 3, the more conducive your initial environment will be to supporting the collaboration. If one or two aspects of your environment are weak, you'll need a plan to address them, or you risk everything coming undone down the track. Scoring well on step 2 is perhaps most important, with the result of step 1 coming second – with strong goodwill and value for the outcome, resourcing issues can usually be resolved.

Once you get a feel for this particular tool, you can use the three variables of value, goodwill and resources to quickly go and take the temperature of your collaboration support in any situation, be it larger-scale and more planned out, or smaller and spontaneous.

This assessment is all the more powerful when combined with an understanding of the level of collaboration at which you're engaging. For example, if you happen to have a roomful of executives whom you suspect distrust one another (representative level), and you only have them for half an hour, I'd advise against taking a collaborative approach. The formalities and history of many executive cultures will likely preclude any amount of genuine collaboration in that time frame, and may even catalyse participants' mistrust of one another and the proposed collaborative process.

A Note on Informal Collaborative Settings

If your collaborative setting tends towards informal – for example, a project with your community, family or friends, rather than with a business or other organisation – you'll want to scale back the formality of your approach too. Sending out calendar invitations for meetings, setting agendas and taking notes are all fairly standard practices at work, but they might feel a little out of place in a lounge room.

Indeed, we often enjoy our more community-based interactions precisely because of their informality. But this can present challenges if you're proposing a collaboration of significant complexity. If this is the case, take it slowly and softly at the outset, allowing plenty of time for participants to get comfortable working with one another while coming to their own realisations regarding the need for shared processes, tools and culture.

This is especially important when there isn't an organisation or job that's holding the participants together in the early stages of collaboration. Without the binding effects of professional reputations and the expectations of bosses, people tend to vote with their feet, moving on quickly when things start to feel awkward or hard. This is often the reality within volunteering and community settings, which creates much frustration for the committed. Producing simple external reference points, such as statements of intent, catchphrases, shared plans and the like, can help considerably. But there are no short-cuts to maintaining the feeling of authenticity needed to keep participants relaxed and comfortable.

I've learned a lot about these dynamics through my own family's efforts to hold annual reunions. After my paternal grandfather passed away, my father and his four siblings realised that this man had played a key role in bringing the whole family together each year, and that this role now had to be filled. But instead of tasking an individual with this responsibility, they chose to take on the job as a group – they decided to collaborate. The main reason for this is that, over the course of several decades, these annual reunions have grown and grown, and they now bring together a family that spans three generations. And as the number of participants has increased – at last count, to about 40 – so too has the complexity of organising the event and aligning all of the participants' needs and interests. A range of tools, such as spreadsheets, voting processes and online collaboration platforms, are now used to coordinate everything from dates and venues to meals and activities.

This level of formality can feel overwrought to anyone new to the get-togethers, but a day or two into a reunion and they quickly realise how much it's needed. The group is distributed across the continental United States and other regions of the world, and different family members have different levels of financial means, as well as time, location and accommodation needs. There are young children and babies to consider. There are various dietary requirements (two of my boys have coeliac disease). The different generations have vastly different activity preferences. And on top of all of this, there's the ever-important reunion T-shirt to produce!

Unsurprisingly, the process is not foolproof. In fact, a few years back, cracks began appearing, with folks feeling like the whole thing was just not working as well as it used to. Then, at a recent reunion, I was asked to facilitate a family meeting to discuss and explore these emerging difficulties. The 'elders' – my dad and his siblings – voiced the challenges they faced in shouldering the lion's share of organisational work for a spiralling number of participants. This raised a simple but confronting question: could the younger generations, many of which have young families and demanding jobs (myself included), take on more of the work, in order to help everyone continue to enjoy the deeply meaningful experiences that the reunions were providing?

Throughout this conversation, I used quite formal but standard facilitation techniques, like setting an agreed agenda; watching the time and keeping the conversation on track; encouraging contributions from those who were quiet, while keeping louder voices in check; feeding back key points; and drawing out and giving a voice to hard topics. That I was able to use these more-formal processes in this informal setting was testament to the collaborative capability our family group has cultivated over nearly 20 years of reunions. Despite it feeling awkward at times, and challenging for those involved, the formality gave the elders the space and validation they needed – to share that it was getting too hard for them to do one of the most important things in their lives, that they needed help, and that the younger generations would need to take responsibility for the reunions in the coming years.

Even the very simple collaboration design I used to facilitate this family conversation required an assessment of the group's collaborative capability. If this had not been the case, the more-formal approach I used would likely have been met with discomfort, possibly even hostility. And if I'd used a more-informal, less-structured approach, we may not have gotten to the heart of the matter.

Even before I developed this design, I'd made a conscious decision to do so. It's unlikely that I would've said 'No' in response to a direct request for help from my dad. However, I still went through the internal process of considering my own interests, and weighing this up along with the opportunities and challenges. And this is often the case in collaboration: even if we feel that there's really no alternative to saying 'Yes', our internal critique of the situation still makes us assess the decision. Being consciously aware of this process helps you develop a better response to the situation.

Tool 4: The Shared Capability Baseline

This tool is designed to help you assess which collaborative capabilities are present or lacking from the start, in order to inform your collaboration decision. It does this by drawing on the missing chair, team and elephant themes covered in Chapter 3 and which are central to the third principle of collaboration: shared capability. For new groups or new projects, shared capability must always be built at the outset from the ground up. It then continues to grow as a group works and learns together.

By way of a reminder, the missing chair represents a lack of shared understanding regarding the meaning of the word 'collaboration' and what it implies when used in a specific situation; the missing team highlights gaps in a group's shared culture and practices; and the missing elephant represents the lack of shared processes, tools and technologies.

STEP 1: ASSESS YOUR SHARED UNDERSTANDING OF COLLABORATION (THE MISSING CHAIR)

Bring to mind your specific collaborative situation or opportunity, and consider in regards to the participants you hope to involve whether there's likely to be a shared understanding of the term 'collaboration'. For example, maybe you worked on a past project together. Did this tell you anything about a common view of collaboration? If you don't have any collaborative history with your prospective participants, can you tell if they're likely to have differing or aligned views on collaboration, due to their backgrounds, personalities or previous experiences?

Based on your responses to these questions, consider the effort that will be needed to align the participants' understanding and expectations of collaboration. Decide if this will be:

1 Difficult (intensive, requiring real work and resourcing)
2 Moderate (involved, requiring dedicated time and focus)
3 Easy (an energising and quick experience)

STEP 2: ASSESS YOUR SHARED CULTURE AND WORK PRACTICES (THE MISSING TEAM)

Do you have a sense of who would comprise the core of your collaboration? These participants will be doing most of the heavy lifting – the cocreation – and will be relied on to 'turn up', whatever this means in your scenario. Consideration of such people will give you a feel for how much, if any, pre-existing collaborative experience, culture or practice connects them. If the core participants have worked together before, this may contribute to some shared capability that can be repurposed to get you started more quickly. If this is the case, look at how much culture and capability can be repurposed. Are there past practices that didn't work so well and need to be reworked or improved?

If you can't tell who's likely to be in the core, the participants probably won't have worked together before. Then you need to decide how much effort will be involved in supporting the individuals to get to know one another, share their experiences of collaboration and expectations, and develop the initial shared working practices. Do you think the participants will value this and contribute time and money if needed?

Based on your responses to these questions and the state of your starting collaborative culture, practice and capabilities, choose an answer that you feel reflects the effort that will be required to cultivate them:

1 Difficult (intensive, requiring real work and resourcing)
2 Moderate (involved, requiring dedicated time and focus)
3 Easy (an energising and quick experience)

STEP 3: SHARED PROCESS, TOOLS AND SYSTEMS (THE MISSING ELEPHANT)

Finally, consider the external structures that will support your collaborative work. Will this work take place within the boundaries of a single organisation or team? If the answer is 'Yes', then there may be readily available tools, systems and processes waiting to support you. If so, will the use of these be a foregone conclusion, or will some negotiation (and therefore time and energy) be required to decide?

Will your collaboration involve or span one or more teams, divisions or organisations? If it will, is there a clear *lead* entity? And will others be expected to adopt that entity's tools, processes and approaches, or those of another organisation? If your collaboration won't involve existing organisations – for example, in a community or artistic setting – will you need to source or create new tools and processes to get your work done?

Different still, your collaboration may be premised on creating a new organisation; for example, a new start-up. If so, will a formal organisational entity, business processes and technology also need to be established, selected or created through collaboration? How intensive is this likely to be? Considering your responses to the above questions, how involved will it be to establish shared tools, systems and processes?

1 Difficult (intensive, requiring real work and resourcing)
2 Moderate (involved, requiring dedicated time and focus)
3 Easy (an energising and quick experience)

STEP 4: SCORE THE CHALLENGE OF ATTAINING ALIGNMENT

Add up the numbers corresponding to your answers above and divide the total by 3. The closer your score is to a 3, the less intensive your collaboration will be, especially in its earlier stages. This in theory represents a collaboration that's more likely to succeed. However, collaborations that require intensive engagement at the outset typically have a high risk/reward profile. While they may be more prone to failure, they also represent higher gains should they succeed. So don't assume you should avoid a collaboration just because this tool has scored it as 'difficult' (a score of between 1 and 2).

Similarly, getting an 'easy' score (of between 2 and 3) doesn't mean that you should collaborate. Carefully consider the results you got from tools 1 through 3. Even 'easy' collaborations take more time and energy than non-collaborative approaches.

Lastly, given your score, consider the likelihood of securing the needed time, resources and commitment to meet these needs. Remember that anything worth doing always seems to take more time, effort and money than you expected!

Tool 5: Space for Collaboration

This tool addresses a final resource that will impact your collaboration decision: the space within which it will take place. I have presented this as a separate concern for several reasons. The first is that space is highly affected by technology, and as a consequence, it often gets tangled up in the expectations we place on technology to solve our problems. These expectations can create false assumptions before we even start, distracting us from the real issues at play – 'If only we had a room with video-conferencing cameras and screens!'

Collaborative space is also multidimensional. It's as much conceptual as it is physical and, increasingly, it's also virtual; for example, a phone call brings people together virtually but not physically (despite how much our phones now seem to be an extension of our bodies). And as human innovation continues apace, the spaces between collaboration participants will continue to fill with technology – even sticky notes are in the process of becoming virtualised! But this doesn't mean that all technologies are equal, or that participants will necessarily use the best technologies, even when these are handed to them on a silver platter.

Yet more-complex dimensions of collaborative space are the interpersonal and intercultural histories that we as participants bring. We may be best friends or archenemies. We may speak the same language and cherish the same holidays, or be so unfamiliar that we may as well be alien creatures from different planets. These differences can create spaces of separation that feel as vast as an ocean, even though we may be standing next to one another.

Yet, despite this potential for distance, there's always the opportunity for remarkable bridges to be built. Recently, I watched as my English-speaking 12-year-old twins built a new friendship and developed several collaborative games with a Spanish-speaking boy of the same age. The primary tool they used was Google Translate via mobile phones borrowed from their parents. Despite none of them ever having used this technology before, they were able to immediately incorporate it into their collaborative problem-solving, communication, and creative production. It was also used as a tool of humour, leading to much fun and joking as the boys sought odd translations and explored funny words. This created a strong connection, and an equally strong friendship.

Space – conceptual and physical – is especially important at the beginning, as it's during the first interactions between founding participants that your collaboration will be at its most vulnerable. Your decision should involve careful consideration of the spaces involved and that you'll need, and their capacity to support your work. You'll also need to consider the role of technology in making or bridging space.

STEP 1: HOW REGULARLY WILL PARTICIPANTS COMMUNICATE AND INTERACT?

Most people will have to *make* time for a collaboration, which means they must be willing to prioritise this. Recalling the participants in your collaboration scenario, do they typically have busy daily schedules, with meetings having to be booked weeks in advance? If so, think carefully about how they might value the proposition for collaboration.

Another impact on interaction occurs when your participants live in different time zones. Dealing with this can be harder than you expect – for example, being based in Australia, I have to carefully plan my work with folks in the United Kingdom, as our business hours usually overlap by only 60 minutes! In these situations, participants will likely need to be able and willing to engage outside of standard work hours.

Similarly, working patterns may need consideration. If half of your participants work night shifts, while the other half work during the day, they'll struggle collectively to share quality time. Living patterns matter too. Stay-at-home parents may find it challenging to collaborate with busy executives or those who have to travel frequently. All of these factors will impact your requirements for collaborative space.

Given their daily living and working patterns, and their willingness to make time, how regularly will your participants be able to interact, whether face to face, by phone, or through other electronic means of communication?

1 Infrequently (1–4 times annually)
2 Occasionally (1–2 times monthly)
3 Frequently (daily to weekly)

STEP 2: HOW MUCH DISTANCE SEPARATES THE PARTICIPANTS?

How much physical space separates your prospective participants? Do they live in different parts of the same town or city, or in different states or countries? Even when participants do live near each other, it can be hard to bring them together if you don't have meeting spaces that are conducive to those people and the activities they'll be involved in. In the next two chapters, we'll look more closely at what types of spaces work well when bringing people together, and the types of activities these spaces need to support. But for the time being, try to imagine one or more spaces that will allow your initial group members to meet face to face.

If you think you'll need to source and hire a physical meeting space, or if significant travel will be involved, can you imagine the participants contributing to this level of resourcing if you aren't able to cover these costs?

Is there any cultural or interpersonal distance that separates your would-be participants? For example, are there significant socioeconomic or cultural differences between them, or do they speak the same language and share the same customs? Are there existing friendships among them, or is there suspicion, mistrust, even enmity? The latter should be thought of as a significant amount of separating space. Also contemplate whether there are any situational issues that might cause separation, such as travel commitments or holidays. Meeting physically is not always necessary – in some cases it's not even desirable – but it's the most powerful way to begin a collaboration.

Given the above considerations, what's your estimation of the distance separating the participants:

1 Significant
2 Moderate
3 Minimal

STEP 3: CAN TECHNOLOGY SUPPORT YOUR COLLABORATION?

Technology can be a powerful force in bridging the space between participants. And to be effective, it doesn't have to be expensive and whiz-bang. Often, the best collaborative technologies are simple, readily available, and low-cost or free, such as phones, email, video-conferencing, instant messaging, and online collaborative documents.

What existing capability and appetite is there likely to be among your participants regarding the use of technology? Do you know what your participants already use or have had experience with in terms of technology? It's reasonable to make some assumptions based on age – older participants will typically feel more comfortable with older forms of technology and have less interest in adopting new forms, while younger participants will be more familiar with newer technologies and be more amenable to learning about them. Given these considerations, overall, do you feel there would be an interest in learning about and using new technologies?

Factoring in the answers to the above questions, can you readily imagine simple and easy-to-use solutions to any of the challenges that stood out in steps 1 and 2 of this tool? For example, regarding the participants who live in different cities or nations, have they had experience with video-conferencing? What about the use of online tools that allow the co-authoring of documents? Might they already use, or be open to trying, group messaging tools?

What's your estimation of the potential of technology (be it old, new, digital, physical, process-based or people-driven) to support communication and collaboration?

1 Low
2 Medium
3 High

STEP 4: CALCULATE HOW CHALLENGING YOUR COLLABORATIVE SPACE NEEDS WILL BE

As before, add up the numbers that correspond to your answers and divide the total by 3. The closer your score is to a 3, the more the initial factors concerning space will support collaboration.

If in step 1 you scored a 1, meaning that participants aren't likely to interact more than several times a year, then beware. As we'll explore in Chapter 12 on growth, the sixth stage of collaboration, frequency of interaction is one of the main enablers of effective teamwork. The momentum generated by regular interaction is essential in overcoming the many other barriers that exist in the first phase of a collaborative initiative.

Scoring low on step 2 – the distance separating participants – is (perhaps counterintuitively) less concerning. Issues of distance can be better addressed by scoring higher on steps 1 and 3. Basically, where there's a will, there's a way – in that there are widely available tools and technologies for bridging the gulf of physical distance. And if people are motivated enough, they're usually able to overcome conceptual distance issues, such as interpersonal and intercultural differences.

Step 3, the ability of technology to support collaboration, is the easiest to overestimate. It's often tempting to believe that a particular technology is the perfect solution to your problems. But add another dash of scepticism before you make any decisions or investments. Establishing any technology almost always takes more time, effort and money than you expect it to.

A Note on Decisions Well Made

Making the conscious decision to collaborate, or not to, is rarely easy. Simply taking more time to consider the decision doesn't necessarily make it any easier, but you'll be more likely to succeed. This is because deciding and doing collaboration both require you to develop a mental model of complex interactions to assess the trade-offs that will inform your design. The sooner you start doing this, the more likely you are to negotiate these with a clear and balanced outlook.

When you've consciously, objectively and personally evaluated an opportunity to collaborate, it should leave you feeling as though you've confronted some tricky considerations. In my experience, the more complex and compelling the collaboration opportunity, the truer this is. This means that when you most need to confront a decision with your eyes wide open, it'll be harder than ever to do so. You'll be tempted to just trust your gut and go on instinct. But while instinct is still an important aspect of decision-making, it shouldn't be the only one.

In particular, watch out for confirmation bias. This is when we seek information or input that validates what we hope to see, as opposed to what's actually there before us. In a collaboration context, this might happen because you especially like the idea of working with a particular individual or organisation. Or it may be that the potential outcome of the collaboration is so exciting that you overlook critical issues with levels of support, capability, or the quality of the collaboration space. Going through the process of applying the five tools I've just described will help you look beyond your biases to see the different factors that could determine success or failure for you.

Regardless of the rigour that you bring to making your decision, the most important part of this first stage of the Collabforge method is to realise that you have a choice, and that you're making it. It's only then that you can grasp the full opportunity to consciously design your collaboration, instead of just letting it happen to you.

CHAPTER 8

Convene

After having said 'Yes' to your collaboration, the next step will be to bring the participants together at least once, if not in an ongoing fashion. This second stage of the methodology helps you to do this by pushing you to think holistically about the entire collaboration. A holistic perspective is important because all the aspects of collaboration are ultimately interdependent. That is, how you might best bring people together for that first conversation is informed by many things: among them, the value proposition for collaboration, your shared understandings and capabilities, the characteristics of your setting, and the specific orientations and personalities of the participants.

To account for these interdependencies, the Collabforge method will show you how to develop a whole plan at the outset, but at low resolution – as you progress and learn, you'll add detail. This will help you assess the many interconnected aspects of the project.

Having what we call a *strawhorse* plan also helps you communicate the value proposition for participation. A strawhorse is a draft of something you want to make that other people can tinker with. You want them to feel comfortable pulling it apart and rebuilding it with you to suit their own visions and interests. When it has finally been reworked, you have a live representation of what people actually want, as opposed to what they say they want. In essence, a strawhorse is collaboration bait – it creates a low bar for involving others, and provides them with something to react to and build on.

When Collabforge started working with the City of Melbourne on their 10-year plan, we created a strawhorse collaboration design that outlined our intentions for the entire process, but didn't specify any detail for the stages and activities beyond the first few. This allowed others to help contribute the missing detail. The success of the FutureMelbourne project was due in large part to this approach – it sent a strong message to people in the organisation that not only were we open to their input, we were actively asking for it.

Our collaboration design also highlighted how we would convene all the participants. While a draft plan would be cocreated by the standard small team within the planning unit, we'd progressively open things up, inviting other internal teams one by one to co-author the plan. This process was to continue until the whole organisation had been invited to participate. Then we'd bring in the key stakeholders, and finally the public at large. This design gave us the ability to take our first steps safely while communicating our intentions, getting feedback and improving the plan as we went.

The first tool in this chapter will take you through a simple process for creating your own high-level collaboration design, as a means for you to develop an understanding of the opportunities and challenges. Throughout the rest of this book, you'll return to this design, iteratively refining it as you learn about collaboration, just as you learn through interacting with others. This is a key feature of collaboration design: the need to continuously revisit and hone the design as a result of outcomes that emerge often unpredictably from the process.

The next four tools will take you through the development of a draft collaboration design that you can use as you convene the first meetings for a collaborative initiative. In preparation for these meetings, the tools will help you consider who should be involved and how, as well as how to best communicate your ideas and the opportunity to participate. The final tool in this chapter will show you how to prepare invitees to meaningfully make their own decisions about whether or not to participate.

Tool 6: A Draft Collaboration Design

A few years ago, I set myself the task of coming up with the simplest possible summary of the key elements of cocreation. The result was the following sentence:

A shared vision guiding active contribution to a shared plan and outcome.

Since I developed this framework, Collabforge has used it in a wide range of contexts, including as a guide to quickly developing a high-level collaboration design. It does this by providing cues for how the core aspects of collaboration work – especially the heart of the process: cocreation.

To begin with, there has to be some kind of shared vision. This can be developed in any number of ways, such as through conversations, meetings, emails, workshops, or by co-authoring a research paper. However it comes about, enough shared vision must be present to align, inspire and cue participants as to where, when and how to act.

This shared vision will guide participants regarding their active contributions towards its realisation. I use the word 'active' here to indicate that participation must involve an input into something that's being jointly created. So adding a sticky note to a whiteboard during a collaborative workshop activity would qualify, whereas sitting passively and listening to a presentation, without asking a question or otherwise interacting, would not.

As the final part of the statement above explains, an active contribution needs to be made to a shared plan and an outcome. Having both in mind when collaborating is imperative for several reasons. Sometimes, a plan can be the outcome of collaboration, its cocreation allowing others to work independently. But providing opportunities for the cocreation *of* the plan (the collaboration design) is the gold standard to aspire to. Those involved will have contributed their insights and interests to how the outcomes are realised. And having helped create the plan, the participants are now invested in its success.

The following steps use these elements – a shared vision, active contribution, and a shared plan and outcome – to frame prompts for developing the initial high-level version of your collaboration design.

STEP 1: CREATE A STRAWHORSE VISION

In regards to your actual or imagined collaboration scenario, write down or simply narrate to yourself an example of what the shared vision might be for your group, in its earliest stages. For example, it might be the design of a new software product that actively incorporates the perspectives and expertise of the software's users. Or it might be an attempt to tackle a particular social issue that requires the participation, insight and influence of all those involved.

Regardless of your particular focus, don't worry about getting this perfect. Just try to jot down a vision for what you're trying to achieve through collaboration, in words that you feel comfortable saying.

STEP 2: PLAN FOR ACTIVE CONTRIBUTION

For this second step, again, write down or simply say to yourself the first thing that you would do with participants. How does the vision developed in step 1 guide them into active contribution? For the first activity, this might be as simple as an informal discussion with participants to refine and build out these ideas.

Now do the same for your second activity. Again, keep things simple and high-level. This could be a second meeting or workshop that involves more participants. Or the aim might be to collaboratively draft a discussion document that consolidates the ideas raised in the initial discussion.

STEP 3: DESIGN FOR SHARED PLANS AND OUTCOMES

Next, consider what a shared plan might look like for your initiative. What format will it be in and how will it be shared? For example, it could be a simple document that's emailed around, or content in an online project-management tool. Also consider how you'll maintain your plan, to ensure you're tracking well and can correct your course when necessary.

As a second part of this step, contemplate and list the outcomes your collaboration might deliver. Consider these outcomes from as many different perspectives as possible, such as tangible outputs (products, documents and so on), learning opportunities, relationships, or experiential benefits (inspiration, excitement and travel). Now, as you did in the previous steps, jot down some quick notes or just verbalise your thoughts.

When you've completed all three steps, review your answers to see if they adequately align with and reinforce each other. Does your vision feel like it will inspire active engagement? Do your ideas concerning a shared plan – what it will look like, how it will be developed and maintained – feel realistic? Do your outcomes feel compelling, and do they help realise your vision?

Tool 7: The Why-How-What Pitch

Now that you have a high-level draft collaboration design, let's put it into a more communicable format. The first step in getting anyone interested and involved in your collaboration is to communicate your ideas in a clear and compelling way.

There are many ways to communicate an idea. We're going to use an approach that specifically does a great job of delivering the right level of detail needed to make an impact. At Collabforge, we call it The Why–How–What Pitch. This format was first made popular by the author and speaker Simon Sinek in his TED talk 'How Great Leaders Inspire Action', in which he reveals a fantastically simple and effective means of conveying the most important aspects of something in a way that inspires your audience to action. We've reworked it to cater to the particular needs of collaboration, as opposed to Simon's original and more general focus on marketing and communication.

Using this framework, we'll create three presentation slides, limiting ourselves to a title and three supporting points for each slide.

STEP 1: WHY IS IT IMPORTANT?

Create a title on this first slide for your collaboration, preferably less than five words. Now develop three supporting points, each point *no more* than one short sentence – ideally just a phrase. Do this by expanding on the vision you created in Tool 6: A Draft Collaboration Design.

The challenge here is to stay focused on the question 'Why?' by digging into the values and beliefs your vision represents. If you aren't sure about this, read your slide title and ask yourself, 'Why do I care and why is it important?' Once you've arrived at a new, deeper answer, ask yourself the same question, repeating this process until you're focused on the heart of the matter.

Your title and its three supporting points shouldn't pull any punches. They are meant to solicit a reaction from your audience. Either they'll say 'Wow, oh yeah!', or 'Whoa, slow down ...' Regardless of whether they're keen to immediately jump on board or they're sceptical, your slides should make a provocative case for cocreation.

STEP 2: HOW WILL IT HAPPEN?

Describe in the second slide how you'll deliver your collaboration – again, limit yourself to a title and three dot-points. You might describe the principles that are essential to realising your vision; for example, being open and transparent, or user-centred. You might also describe a particular method or approach that you feel strongly about, like user-centred design, or cocreation.

The trick in this step is to focus on process and principles over activities and outputs (which are dealt with in step 3). Just be aware that, as there are many ways of getting something done, the particular approach you adopt will influence both the types of activities you use and the outcomes you generate. For example, I might take a holiday with my family to Tahiti, but flying there in a jet will get very different outcomes for our holiday than if we sailed to Tahiti in a boat. You can also consider this your strategy: the way of being, thinking and acting that will deliver on your vision.

STEP 3: WHAT DOES IT LOOK LIKE?

In this final step, get specific about what you'll do and deliver. Focus on the key activities that will drive your collaboration, and the tangible outputs that will produce the most value. Remember, this isn't meant to be the final word on the matter, but rather a strawhorse for prospective participants to pull apart and rebuild with you.

Again limiting yourself to a simple title and three dot-points, zoom into the things you'll actually do and produce. Try to give your participants a feeling for what they'll be doing, as well as what they'll get out of the collaboration.

Developing three simple slides may feel like a vast oversimplification of your concepts. But that's the point of this tool. By concentrating your ideas and the opportunity into a tiny little shot that can be delivered to an audience in only a few minutes, you can deliver a powerful impact. I learned this concept when I was studying kung-fu. A blow delivered with less surface area means a greater impact, without exerting any additional energy. (My Chinese-born and -trained kung-fu teacher could give you a poke with his finger that was far more painful than the average person's punch!)

To gain all the benefits of this approach, you just need to be accurate. Choose your words carefully and focus on the most important aspects of your pitch, in particular the value proposition it represents for participants.

At Collabforge, we recently used this tool to help an executive develop a whole-of-organisation strategy. The business concerned delivers large human-development programs in developing nations around the world on behalf of the Australian, UK and US governments. This particular executive had been given the task of creating a strategy to leverage the business' existing assets to strongly differentiate it within an increasingly competitive marketplace.

The strategy we developed was clever and exciting, but it was also long-term and complex, and it would need other key executives to support it and participate in it. To achieve this, we distilled the findings from six months of interviews and workshops with staff, along with a substantive strategy document, into the Why–How–What three-slide format. We used these slides to kick off a focused conversation with a dozen or so executives who'd flown in from around the world, where we quickly zeroed in on their key concerns. We then took the executives through a few cocreation activities (outlined in Chapter 9) that helped them to pull apart aspects of our strategy so that we could reconstruct it with them as a group. This allowed them to sense-check and improve our ideas while building a shared understanding with us of the strategy. The result was resounding support for and approval of the budget needed to deliver the collaboration across the organisation over the next three years.

Tool 8: Participant Mapping for the Core, Community and Crowd

Before delivering your Why–How–What Pitch, as detailed in Tool 7, you'll want to think through who will be included, and in what way. You'll want to include some people on a regular basis to help make decisions and discover opportunities. Others you may need mainly for approvals and formal support. Still others you'll want to keep in the loop to make sure they remain supportive advocates of the project, or in case you want to involve them more closely later on. Understanding what the participant make-up will be creates another important part of your strawhorse.

This tool utilises the second principle of collaboration, shared process, which was introduced in Chapter 6. This principle stipulates that three interrelated social processes are involved in collaboration: cocreation, cooperation and coordination. We'll use each of these processes to initially map participants and stakeholders, creating a cross-section of your collaboration that focuses on what their levels of involvement and roles could be (see Figure 5).

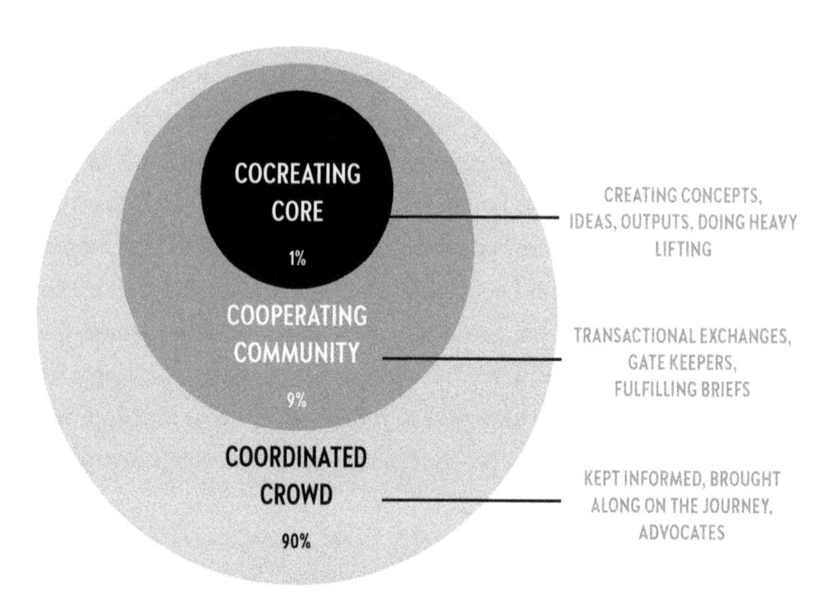

Figure 5. The Anatomy of Collaboration

In any collaborative effort that's larger than a handful of people, you'll have a *cocreating core* that meets more regularly than the extended group. They tend to get the day-to-day work done and, as a result, they're more engaged in cocreation with one another than with other participants. Due to the intensity and time required of its members, this group is often the smallest of the three sub-groups.

Beyond this core, there's usually a group that contributes in a more-transactional manner – generally from the perspective of a decision-maker, providing a 'Yes' or 'No' for high-impact or risky choices. They can also fulfil the briefs designed by the core; for example, creating the branding or logo for your new collaborative enterprise. This *cooperating community* can more easily scale than the core, as their contributions require less social negotiation and effort to integrate.

Finally, the largest group tends to be the *coordinated crowd*, comprising people who know about your initiative but aren't necessarily committed to it or signed up to contribute anything specific. These folks play an important role as advocates for you, providing moral support or even referrals. For example, in conversation with someone else, they might mention you and your initiative favourably; they may even direct opportunities that arise in such conversations back to you.

The boundaries between these three groups are almost always porous, with participants moving fluidly between them. Often, as part of your collaboration design, you'll plan for this movement. You might want to bring someone into your coordinated crowd so that they're all warmed up when you're ready to ask them into the cooperating community. Similarly, someone might participate in the cocreating core for a defined period, after which they'll move out to the coordinated crowd.

This tool requires you to create a list for each of these three categories. Do your best to imagine which individuals, groups and organisations will be involved in your collaboration and put them in the relevant list. While this initial draft should focus on how you think things might start out, also jot down any movements between the groups that you hope for or anticipate.

COCREATING CORE

1 {Participant group or individual one}
2 {Participant group or individual two}

COOPERATING COMMUNITY

1 {Participant group or individual three}
2 {Participant group or individual four}

COORDINATED CROWD

1 {Participant group or individual five}
2 {Participant group or individual six} ...

After creating a list like the one above, consider the implications of being unable to get a participant into the group you want. For example, would your project still be viable if a key person was willing to participate at the cooperative level – providing discrete inputs, but only when cued to do so within a predescribed scope – but not in the core?

Also give consideration to those whom we might call *influencers*: people or organisations that, for whatever reason, hold sway over others whom you hope to involve. They may also be seen as influential by those whom you hope your initiative will ultimately impact, such as a particular community or customer segment. Or they may be people who are simply well regarded by those you want to involve. Never underestimate the importance and pull-power of influencers. Winning one over may be the key to attracting the talent you need.

A few years back, Collabforge assisted the administration of a city to design and develop an innovation lab. This was to be a new type of business function that would help evaluate and develop new ideas coming from either staff or the community. Nothing like this had ever been tried before in this city, and we were very conscious of the risk that the broader internal leadership wouldn't understand the value of the project. As we developed our stakeholder map, we realised that we'd need significant influence and support from executive-level staff to help others, including councillors, the mayor and the CEO, defend the budget of the innovation lab for at least several years.

We quickly identified the CIO and his director as the right people for this job. However, we just as quickly realised that to get and maintain the necessary buy-in, we'd need to have these two people see the initiative as their own. That meant they'd have to play a part in its cocreation and be involved in our core team. But how could we ever get enough of their time so that they could be meaningfully involved at that level?

To solve this problem, we added the two executives to our cooperating community, as would be generally done for leaders, involving them in key transactional decision-making and review processes. In addition, we also held a monthly deep-dive strategy meeting with them, where we cocreated solutions to problems we encountered along the way. During these meetings, we reviewed our progress and collaboratively revised the evaluation framework that the executives held us accountable to. This helped maintain alignment with the shifting strategic priorities coming from the city council and the mayor, a perspective that our project team would never have had access to without the CIO and his director's participation.

Through this 'half-in-the-core' approach, the CIO and his director developed a deep understanding and sense of shared ownership of the initiative. Crucially, they became significantly more personally invested in the project. As a result, this innovation lab still exists today, having weathered numerous restructures and changes in executive personnel as well as in the city's political leadership.

Tool 9: The Double-Sided Value Proposition

Knowing who you want to involve, and in what way, doesn't mean you can convince those people to participate: that's what your Why–How–What Pitch is for. But it's wise to bring a little more clarity to how you'll pitch to particular groups and individuals. They'll almost certainly have differing value propositions that will determine whether or not they'll jump on board.

To develop a value proposition for someone which you can test and refine, you need to build a mental model of them: what they care about and why, how they'll likely react to different ideas and situations, and so on. This tool lets you dig into the motivations and interests of those you'll engage. Specifically, you'll try to untangle their interests from your own – it seems to be a feature of human nature to regard the perspectives of others as versions of our own perspective. This is especially the case when you try to imagine why others would want to participate in something you're excited about. Almost without fail, you'll project your own value proposition for a collaboration onto those of prospective participants.

The Double-Sided Value Proposition (or DSVP, as we like to call it at Collabforge) first gets you to make explicit your own value proposition, then do the same for your participants – simply fill in Table 1 to do this. Now look at the collaboration from the perspective of each participant and consider what they might get out of it. You'll probably find that your perspective is easy to jot down, whereas your participants' require a little more consideration. This is the primary point of this tool, so take your time and be thoughtful about your answers.

	VP 1: My value proposition for their participation	VP 2: Their value proposition for participation
Participant/Group 1	...	...
Participant/Group 2	...	...

Table 1. The Double-Sided Value Proposition

As you complete this table, just remember that motivations for participation are multidimensional. Participants may focus on the project itself, but they may be more interested in building specific relationships or skills through their involvement, or seek a bump to their reputation and credibility.

Add as many rows as you need to for different participants or groups. What differentiates one from another varies from collaboration to collaboration, so go further than the core, community and crowd groupings. Just give it some thought and differences will stand out. For example, some participants might contribute more based on their technical expertise, while others might bring significant resources. Yet others might be of a different type; for example, a government partner versus someone from the private sector. Just remember that what earmarks a separate grouping for this activity is whether or not they have a significantly unique value proposition for participation.

Take this opportunity to also consider the potential of your vision. Be creative and try to imagine what your participants' interest *could* be in its realisation. You may be able to suggest compelling reasons for involvement that they wouldn't otherwise have thought of, which can streamline and incentivise their participation.

Once you have a draft DSVP, you can test it as part of your straw-horse collaboration design. Simply state your two value propositions and ask the participants for their feedback, along these lines: 'I would like your participation because [*your* value propositions for their participation (VP 1)]. I feel you might be interested in participating because [*their* value propositions (VP 2)]. But this is just my best guess. Have I got this right?'

Gaining a response to this question will give you one of the most powerful inputs you can get in regards to bringing people together: a validated value proposition.

Tool 10: The Ask

This tool creates a focused *ask* of prospective participants, to directly confirm if they're willing to come together to explore the collaboration opportunity. The ask is singled out here because it's important to strike a balance between being focused and specific, while not pushing too far or too hard. If you get this balance just right, people can weigh things up based on what they've heard and discussed so far, then make a decision on collaborating. (Notice how, in doing so, you're helping participants with the first stage of collaboration: deciding whether to do it.)

However, more often than not, they'll want to understand a little more before agreeing to collaborate. They may have ideas regarding others they'd like to involve, and on how the vision might be reshaped to generate a stronger value proposition for these people, or themselves. Usually, they'll want to get a better idea of what the commitment might look like, but they'll need to arrive at this through further discussion of the concept in general.

To account for this, it's a good idea to include in your ask an invitation for the person's reactions and feedback, prior to asking for their commitment to the next step. For example: 'Before we discuss if you would consider attending a meeting with the others whom I've asked to participate, do you have any questions, or any thoughts on who else I might involve or how to improve the concept?'

Now consider where your Why–How–What Pitch ended (what the likely activities and outcomes might be for participants), as well as the results of your DSVP in the previous tool, and write down a specific ask. At this point, keep things fairly short-term, perhaps focusing on asking for involvement in the first activity in your 'What' slide.

You may be able to create one ask for everyone you anticipate speaking to as a first step, and in many respects this is a good idea. However, it's equally OK to create several asks for different participants or groups. The important thing is that you've thought through exactly what you're asking for in your early conversations, and how this will impact your prospective participants.

Tool 11: Inputs to Your First Group Discussion

The previous four tools are designed to provide a number of inputs to your first interactions with would-be participants, catering to a range of situations, whether they are phone calls, meetings or workshops, designed to get people on board your collaboration. However, a few more inputs may be needed to adequately prepare participants.

Each step of this tool focuses on a different aspect of such an event, so that you can determine what information is important to provide ahead of a first interaction, as well as what level of detail it should convey. That said, this tool can be used *anytime* you need to prepare to bring people together.

STEP 1: WHY ARE WE COMING TOGETHER?

Consider the following questions and select a low/medium/high rating for each:

1. How complex is the subject matter or outcome you're trying to achieve as a group?
2. How big a commitment will participants need to make to be part of the initiativc?
3. How unfamiliar will participants be with one another, and/ or how much tension (of any type) may exist between them?

The higher the rating for each of these questions, the more information you should consider providing to address the question 'Why are we coming together?' At the 'lower' end of the spectrum, a title for your meeting that reflects the initiative may be enough, especially if you've delivered some version of your pitch to all of those invited. At the 'higher' end, you could provide your Why–How–What Pitch slides, and even some of your talking points. You can also flesh these out into a one-page brief for the session.

STEP 2: HOW WILL THE SESSION BE RUN?

Answer the following questions:

1 How many participants will be involved?
2 How many topics or concepts will the group need to work through?
3 Will there be an external or dedicated facilitator?

If your answers to questions 1 and 2 err towards 'Many', then consider providing agenda topics or focus questions for the meeting. If there are only a couple of participants, or if the topics or concepts are fairly straightforward, you can probably get away with little to no information about how the session will be run.

If you answered 'Yes' to question 3, you should flag this with the group so that they're prepared for a facilitator to manage the discussion. Ideally, you should introduce the facilitator by name and background in your invitation.

STEP 3: WHAT SHOULD PARTICIPANTS DO TO PREPARE?

Now answer these questions:

1 Will the subject matter be unfamiliar to the participants, wholly or in part?
2 Will they need to have made any decisions or reached any conclusions before arriving?
3 Will mutual goodwill or appreciation significantly increase if the participants learn more about one another before meeting?

If you answered 'Yes' to questions 1 or 2, you should consider providing additional background reading prior to the meeting. This could inform the context of your collaboration, or it could focus on the subject matter involved. If you also answered 'Yes' to question 3, it might be further background on some or all of the participants, especially if there's something notably relevant to your collaboration that others may not be aware of.

Keep in mind that there's a good chance that whatever you provide ahead of the meeting will not get a full or in-depth review. So try not to make an appraisal of the preparation materials mandatory. Rather, this input should be more about helping participants feel comfortable and ready to engage. Keep the materials light, focused and to the point. Preference diagrams, images and video over pages of text. If detailed reports are involved, provide executive summaries, or page references to help participants jump to the relevant sections.

STEP 4: WHEN WILL IT HAPPEN?

Answer the following questions:

1. How difficult will it be to find a time that works for everyone?
2. How busy is the time of year when the meeting is being held? For instance, is it near the end of the financial year or holidays?
3. How much lead time do you have between your individual pitch discussions and bringing the people together?

If you answered 'Very' to questions 1 or 2, then you'll have to work hard to find a time when everyone can meet. Even if the participants aren't so busy and it's a relatively calm time of year, I always try to allow 2–3 weeks to pin down a date for when I'd like the meeting to happen by. Allow even more time if you're constrained by having only one option for your meeting date or have a particularly large group.

If there's more than a month of lead time between your initial discussions and the group convening (question 3), then you should plan to give the participants one or two reminders. At a minimum, provide a reminder two weeks before the meeting, at the same time highlighting any preparation you'd like them to do. Consider not providing preparation materials until this point, to maximise their attention.

STEP 5: WHERE WILL IT BE HELD?

Answer the following questions:

1. How difficult will it be to get a location that works for everyone?
2. How far will participants need to travel, or how unfamiliar will the location be?
3. How challenging will navigation to the venue be, or, if it's an online meeting, how unfamiliar might the participants be with the technology?

If you answered 'Very' for one or more of these questions, provide more rather than less detail and support when it comes to finding the space and getting oriented. There's nothing worse than starting a group meeting and having stragglers arrive late and annoyed because they got confused and stressed out trying to find the venue. If it's a challenging place to find – for example, it's somewhere on a large university campus – provide step-by-step navigation instructions and put up signs. Also provide phone numbers for people to contact should they run into trouble.

If the space is to be in digital form, or if the meeting will occur via a conference call, make sure you've tested the system yourself – better yet, consider asking attendees to do a test run themselves before the meeting. If the technology requires users to log in, create accounts, download software, or simply use something they've never used before, add at least 10–15 minutes to your agenda to get everyone present and ready to start.

Above all, your focus on preparing and providing inputs for participation should demonstrate deep respect for people's time and effort, setting the stage for this respect to be reflected back at you in the meeting itself. This doesn't mean you have to go overboard, but do take it seriously. Never underestimate the disruptive potential of social anxiety!

For these reasons, for larger collaborations where there are many participating organisations or groups, consider breaking up this stage into a few steps. For example, if key influencers are going to affect whether or not a larger group is on board, then you might run a shorter, less-formal session with them beforehand. You might do likewise if different groups hold significantly different perspectives or starting points. Breaking up a larger group meeting into smaller separate ones can lower the initial social tensions for those meeting for the first time, making it easier to achieve your outcomes.

If you do take this staged approach, be careful not to undermine trust by giving the impression that you're having secret conversations or prioritising 'more important' participants over others. Be transparent with the larger group about who you've met with, why you met them, and what the outcomes were. In my experience, people are typically happy for you to meet with groups progressively, as ultimately it does some of the collaborative work for the overall group, making it easier for later participants to join in.

A Note on Choosing the Right Meeting Space

The space you choose for your first and/or subsequent interactions can significantly impact the participants' experience, thereby shaping their view of your collaboration opportunity. This goes for online spaces as much as for those in the real world. The space you collaborate within will also affect the type and quality of the contributions. So it's important to think carefully about what kind of space will best support the group interactions you have in mind.

Consider using a space that's neutral or even new to most of the participants. This means no-one will have the advantage of being on home ground. It can even become a talking point, helping to loosen social stiffness: 'That's a very interesting sculpture in the foyer ...' or 'Wow, look at that view!' These things might seem trivial, but they facilitate subtle yet important ways in which people can begin bonding.

A meeting space itself is also a form of technology that can serve any number of functions, such as providing shelter, comfort and light. Within it, whiteboards and data projectors can be essential for realising the first principle of collaboration: shared ideas. *Showing* a group what they are thinking encourages shared ideas to form more quickly and easily. (These devices are important in regards to many of the group activities presented in Chapter 9.)

Also consider aspects like seating and a room's layout. The ability to move tables and chairs around, creating different configurations to suit specific activities, can be of great benefit.

By now, you should have all the key elements you need to successfully convene your first meetings, with the goal of getting a group excited to collaborate. You now need to decide how to best use these elements, based on your specific situation. Some tools will have done most of their work as you created them; for example, Tool 6: A Draft Collaboration Design. Others, like the slides from Tool 7: The Why–How–What Pitch, provide a useful presentation for participants in that first meeting. However you bring these elements together, the crucial outcome is to clearly communicate a compelling opportunity for collaboration by focusing on the value propositions of your participants. In the next chapter, we'll focus on specific activities that support cocreation – the engine that will ultimately drive your value proposition.

CHAPTER 9

Cocreate

If you're designing a large, complex collaboration, you'll probably want to begin running some cocreation activities in your first few meetings. If so, you need to consider how to streamline things in order to get to work and start making progress as soon as possible. That said, it can be hard to know where to start with a large group, particularly as there's often an excess of social discomfort and self-consciousness. Fortunately, the tools in this chapter will help you overcome these early challenges.

Even when you're working with smaller collaborative groups, getting started can still be a challenge. This is because, whether your group is small or large, the first stage of a collaboration is typically characterised by what I refer to as a 'cold start'. A warm engine starts much more easily than a cold one, but if the members of your group have never before created together, collectively they'll be at their coldest. Once the participants have a little cocreation under their belt, and a better understanding of each other and how they all work together, things will flow much more naturally.

The first tool in this chapter will help you achieve this by providing a runsheet template for organising all the information you need to run any collaborative activity. Tools 13 through 18 then provide a range of specific activities and techniques you can deliver in your early collaborative sessions. We've used these tools hundreds of times at Collabforge as they have been specifically designed to get a group aligned and off to a warm start with a range of low-risk collaborative experiences.

The last two tools in this chapter detail activities that will redirect your group's cocreation focus from your subject matter towards the collaboration design you built out in Chapter 8. This will have the effect of continuing to build your group's collaboration capability and improving your design by getting your collaborators' input, while increasing their shared ownership and buy-in.

Tool 12: The Facilitation Runsheet

A cornerstone of the Collabforge method is that you must always resource the job of facilitation. It might be done formally or informally by an external expert or yourself, or shared around a number of people. However you do it, just make sure it gets done. Facilitation is an element of the third principle of collaboration: shared capability. It helps to bridge the capability gaps that participants may have, especially at the beginning of collaboration, while improving their ability to focus on the task at hand. Facilitation is its own art and science, and I highly recommend that you seek out further resources and training in this area if it's something you plan on doing a lot of.

Developing a detailed plan for a session, what we call a *runsheet*, is one of the best aids in both planning for and facilitating your session. A great runsheet plays two roles: before your session, it helps you confirm that you have the right activities to generate the outcomes you need; and during your session, it helps you to stay focused on delivering these outcomes, while keeping to the time allotted.

This tool captures the key aspects of the runsheet that we use at Collabforge for designing and delivering a group session of any sort.

Table 2 presents these aspects within an example of what a runsheet might look like once it's filled in.

Title: Collaboration Workshop Date: 4 May 2022 Outcome: Understanding and agreement to commence the initiative					
Time	Outcome	Activity	Inputs	Output	Notes
9:00am - 9:30am (30min)	Room set up & tech tested	Organise chairs & tables Post signage Test data projector Clean off whiteboard Sticky notes, markers & water on table	Room signage Sticky notes & markers Whiteboard markers, erasers Water	Nil	Address is ... Check in with reception to get access to room
9:30am - 10:05am (35min)	Participants welcomed, situated, introduced to one another	9:30 - 9:45: Welcome, settling in, and time for late arrivals 9:45 - 10:00: Round-robin introductions 10:00 - 10:05: Discuss agenda	Participant list (names and organisations)	Nil	Jane Smith said she might be running 10 minutes late
10:05am - 10:30am (25min)	Shared understanding of purpose & concepts confirmed	10:05 - 10:15: Why-How-What Pres. 10:15 - 10:30: Clarifications & discussion	Presentation slides Data projector	Key questions listed	Ask everyone if the agenda makes sense Ask for clarifications only (limit discussion as we will dive into ideas in next segment)

Table 2. Sample Runsheet

You'll notice that the outcomes are listed at the top of the table and prioritised in each row, second only to the time of the particular activity. This approach of leading with outcomes can be applied to design tasks of almost any type. When following this approach, first suspend all planning on what you'll do and how you'll do it, until you're clear on why you're doing it and what you're hoping to deliver as a result. This means that, as you run your activity, regardless of the twists and turns that may take place, you can stay focused on the goal – to get the outcomes, not necessarily to finish a given activity.

Setting your outcomes as the goal and staying focused on them is important because collaborative conversations, activities and their conclusions can be unpredictable, often requiring improvisation to stay on track. This may seem at odds with developing a detailed runsheet, but thinking through the facilitation details beforehand will help you make course corrections in the moment by giving you something to edit and with which to remain grounded. You'll also have everything in place, logistically speaking, so that you can spend more of your time, energy and focus on what matters: a quality experience for those in the room that delivers the outcomes you need.

At Collabforge, we often develop the outcomes for a runsheet collaboratively with our clients. We start with the outcome for the entire session, then work our way to an understanding of the sub-outcomes that will deliver on the overall outcome. This allows us to check that we're on the same page as the client, and that we're meeting their needs and expectations. We then select or develop activities with these outcomes in mind, in a less-collaborative fashion, by directing the design in accordance with our many years of experience.

If you're planning on convening your group online, a runsheet will help you in the same way as for a face-to-face session. While you may not have physical space factors to consider, managing technology can be equally time-consuming and challenging, if not more so. Make sure you've allowed enough time to address this. Also remember that, whether the meeting is online or offline, the details addressed in your runsheet should increase the more formal the context, or the more people are involved.

Even if there are only two or three people participating, go through the process of listing all the outcomes you need, starting with the overall session outcome. Organise them in an order that makes sense from the perspective of how they must be generated, and how one flows into the next. Now put times and activities against them. Lastly, list any inputs needed for the activities (materials created beforehand and used to run an activity), as well as any outputs the activities should produce (tangible results of the activity process).

Once you have a first draft of your runsheet, step through it in its entirety, imagining the activities and the people in the room. Play it out in your mind as if it's happening. Ask yourself what might these folks say or do, and how will others react. Ask yourself if you need to reorder any of the activities. What might go wrong? How realistic are the time estimations? What will you need at hand for things to run smoothly (materials, a glass of water, and so on). As you think through these aspects, jot down key insights in the 'Notes' column.

Prompting you to simulate in your mind all the participants moving through the activities, with the outcomes and outputs being generated, is one of the most important things this tool will do. You need to be able to feel your plan working as you run your mental simulation. If you can't, dig into why and make changes to your runsheet accordingly. Add more detail if needed. Keep refining it until you can really imagine it all coming together in your mind's eye.

Tool 13: Individual Perspectives

It's very important that you understand the perspectives of your fellow participants, especially in your early working sessions and meetings. This creates a foundation for shared understanding, shared process and goodwill, the ingredients of great collaboration. On the flipside, not taking the time to do this significantly increases the likelihood of confusion and conflict as your collaboration progresses.

The following tool will help you begin your meetings or workshops with the participants by learning about each other's perspectives, interests, expectations and assumptions. It will help your group maintain a focused conversation while drawing out important ideas and perspectives in a relatively short time.

STEP 1: INDIVIDUALLY ANSWER QUESTIONS

This activity starts with participants individually answering a set of questions. Below I've listed a set of standard questions that you can use, but before relying on them, take the time to think through what other questions might draw out the most important perspectives for your particular collaboration. These questions typically work best when they're asked of everyone, to create a common platform and experience for all involved.

1 What's your name and (if relevant) your organisation and role?
2 What most interests you about the proposed initiative?
3 What do you see as the biggest challenges and opportunities?

For more-complex collaborations, consider adding a question that emphasises the subject matter. Another approach is to directly ask participants if any 'compelling questions' come to mind that everyone should respond to. If so, just add these to the list.

Give the participants 2–5 minutes to write down their answers, without discussing them with anyone, before undertaking the next step. It's important to give them this time to think reflectively and write before speaking – you want them to provide considered insights to the group, not simply perfunctory responses. So make sure most people have completed the task before moving to step 2.

STEP 2: SHARE YOUR ANSWERS

When sharing answers to the above questions, work your way around the group. And if the group is large, ask each participant to keep their response succinct. That's because if, for instance, there are 20 participants, and each one takes two minutes to give their answer, then 40 minutes will be eaten up before your session has even started! If I feel that this step is especially important, but I'm worried about how long it might take, I'll start up a visible timer and tell everyone they have 60 seconds. This allows people to self-manage their time. Also, I'll usually go first in this situation to set an example.

If you have a very large group, say 30 or more people, consider having them share their answers in smaller groups, or across tables if the seating allows for this. I've run this activity with groups of several hundred participants, with great results, having accepted that the best we can do is to have those who are seated together learn more about one another.

Regardless of how you manage the process of sharing these answers, avoid diving into conversation at this point. The aim is simply to get the various perspectives out and to let everyone make their own judgements about what it all means.

STEP 3: DISCUSS AND REFLECT

This last step of the group discussion tool is optional. I recommend it for collaborations that are larger or more complex, or if the participants are unfamiliar with one another, or their perspectives are likely to be significantly different.

After everyone has had the chance to share their answers to the questions (see step 2), make time for some open discussion. Invite the participants to reflect on what they've heard, and ask if any new challenges or opportunities have been suggested. Take note of insights or tensions that you feel might be worth returning to. You can even capture these on a whiteboard.

A Note on Modelling Behaviour

A collaborative group's first conversations can feel a little awkward as participants try to get comfortable with one another. This is normal and to be expected. Absorbing this awkwardness is a key role of the facilitator, who can do this by being the first one to share, thereby breaking the ice. Energy and attitude (both positive and negative) are infectious, so if you're facilitating, try to model the behaviour you're hoping for. You may need to give your tone and body language a little boost if you yourself are feeling shy and awkward. This will help the group to feel more comfortable and relaxed, making these first interactions more effective and efficient.

Tool 14: The Why-How-What Discussion

Once the participants are together, be it physically or virtually, and they're getting a feel for each other's perspectives and orientations, you can start establishing the foundation of shared understanding needed for cocreation. To assist you, this tool merges into a single presentation the outputs from Tool 7: The Why–How–What Pitch, Tool 9: The Double-Sided Value Proposition and Tool 10: The Ask.

Exactly how you bring these elements together will depend on the number of participants and the level of formality they're used to. The more participants and the more formality, the more you need a rehearsed presentation with visuals and preparatory materials. On the other hand, if there's less than a handful of participants and they're already friends, then the only thing you'll need is a few notes to make sure you hit your main points. For the purposes of this tool, let's assume that your collaboration falls somewhere in-between these extremes: there are a dozen or so participants, most of them never having met in a substantive way, and the level of formality is common to most medium-to-large organisations.

STEP 1: CREATE A CONSOLIDATED OVERVIEW

To quickly focus participants on what matters, I recommend starting with the following eight presentation slides:

1. Title/welcome: a simple title slide
2. Context: a handful of key framing points
3. Why: your material from Tool 7
4. How: your material from Tool 7
5. What: your material from Tool 7
6. DSVP: your material from Tool 9, but generalised or adapted for the audience
7. Ask: your material from Tool 10, but reworked as described below
8. Discussion prompt: to be developed as described below

As you pull together slides 1–6, make sure you keep the overview short and punchy – aim for 10–15 minutes, which means no more than two minutes per slide.

Let your ideas speak for themselves and concentrate on the presentation outcome, which is to provide the minimum amount of ideas and information needed for a focused conversation. Try to get to this point as quickly and efficiently as possible. The discussion that follows is your first important activity as a group.

That said, even for very short overviews, it never hurts to spend a little time jazzing up your slides with some nice formatting and images. Certainly don't overload your audience with too much textual content. Keep it lean with roughly three points per slide, each no more than a phrase or a simple sentence. Remember that people can't really read and listen to you talk at the same time – they'll have to choose one over the other.

My own general approach is to read and then briefly elaborate on the points as they appear on-screen. This keeps the audience moving through the content at the same pace as me, while also ensuring that I'm not wasting my breath.

STEP 2: REWORK YOUR ASK AND DEVELOP DISCUSSION PROMPTS

For slide 7, revisit the ask you created as part of Tool 10 and revise as necessary – your thinking may have evolved since then, or you may have a slightly different ask for those now in the room. Present your ask as a concise statement, something like:

The Ask: Meet once a week for one month.
Then decide to continue if we like what we've achieved.

The goal is simply to let the participants know exactly what you're asking of them, letting them take an initial step in their commitment if possible. At the same time, signal to them that you don't need the answer at this particular moment – this is what the overall meeting and discussion are for, helping them inform their choices. To make this clear, you could say something like the following (it doesn't need to be in the slide): 'I'm hoping that through the course of today, you'll get a better understanding of the opportunity and be interested in meeting again as a group'.

Directly following slide 7, begin a discussion by asking if anyone needs a clarification; check if anything didn't make sense, or if more detail is needed on something. Just answer any questions and respond to any requests – don't get drawn into a conversation just yet. If substantive topics arise, simply take note of them and let people know you'll come back to them after the clarifications.

When you think everyone understands, move on to your final slide, which should be titled 'Discussion'. I recommend starting this part of the conversation by picking up any points you set aside during the clarifications. Then ask if there are any challenges or opportunities that immediately stand out. To emphasise this, I add 'Challenges &

Opportunities?' as a dot-point to my discussion slide. This keeps the conversation focused on finding out what things people feel might block their involvement, as well as what interests them most about what you've just presented (their value proposition).

You may have other talking points that you want to address at this time, depending on your initiative. Consider adding these to slide 8 as another dot-point. Having the discussion prompts on the slide also gives you something to refer to if you need to refocus the conversation.

STEP 3: DELIVER YOUR PRESENTATION

When delivering your presentation, keep it on-point and stick to the time allocated, so that you preserve your discussion time and effectively set up the group for a conversation. This discussion is really important because the participants will be engaging in their first cocreation as they share and build on each other's contributions. Don't get in the way of this by feeling you have to respond to every point, or be at the centre of the conversation by raising all the great ideas you've had in the past – there will be time for this later. Rather, encourage the participants to respond to each other in order to catalyse genuine dialogue, even if you know the answer to a question someone has posed. Also draw out participants who've been quiet by giving them an easy point to respond to. And capture any points of value or concern that arise so that everyone can reflect on these down the track.

To finish up, ask if anyone sees any particular issues that might block them from participating. Don't necessarily try to solve these on the spot; just listen and take notes. In these early stages, it's best to take things slowly. You can always do follow-ups with individuals later on.

Tool 15: Ideas on Display

As you might recall from the discussion of the first principle of collaboration (shared ideas) in Chapter 6, the externalisation of ideas is a central part of nearly all substantive collaborations. When we see, hear, touch, smell or taste our ideas in the real world, it triggers different parts of our minds and we think differently about them. We're also able to stay focused on them for longer periods of time, which allows us to think more deeply about them.

This process is especially important in the early stages of a group's formation. As the members start working together, a process of building up and on shared ideas begins. These ideas are layered on each another, so individuals need to confirm one another's views by somehow sensing them tangibly in the real world, otherwise false assumptions are easily made. If this happens, it can create a foundation that consists of misunderstandings and half-formed understandings, or one that lacks any shared understanding at all. Your group will be sitting on a chair with a broken leg, and later on, when the group shifts its weight, you're all likely to fall over.

This tool is designed to make you think about how to keep your participants on the same page whenever a group discussion takes place. While the emphasis here is on the initial phases of cocreation, this practice of 'putting your ideas on display' should be continued. Externalising your group's ideas is often the same thing as getting the work of collaboration done, as typically, your goal will be to cocreate something real in the world. Because of this, the more externalisation becomes a habit for your group, the more your group's productivity will increase.

STEP 1: DECIDE WHAT TO CAPTURE

As a group begins to cocreate, a great deal is often said on the way to finding out what really matters. This can make it hard to decide what to capture. To drive cocreation, focus on capturing what you feel will progress the group's shared understanding towards the creation of shared value. The choice is somewhat subjective. Don't worry about capturing everything – this is not about taking the minutes of a meeting. Gather the points of interest that seem to resonate among the group, or at a minimum the points that relate back to your discussion prompts.

Of particular interest should be key terms and concepts central to your collaboration that are thrown around without much thought, on the assumption that everyone knows what they mean. Think of these as the foundational pillars of your collaboration. There's no harm in checking they're of sound construction before they're fully installed; on the other hand, there can be a good deal of harm done if they turn out to be full of cracks after a substantial structure has been built upon them. Tool 16: Aligned Understandings provides a process dedicated to confirming these core concepts, but just keeping an eye out for them as you capture will do wonders.

STEP 2: DECIDE WHAT MEDIA TO USE

When determining what type of media to use, consider both the environment you're working in and the nature of the conversation you're capturing. For an initial, informal and relatively free-flowing dialogue, a whiteboard is often the perfect option. Not only is the whiteboard inherently collaborative, it allows you to quickly jot down notes, erase and rework ideas, and draw diagrams in a way that few other media permit. However, beware of meeting rooms with pre-installed whiteboards. They may not be well maintained, with a surface that's in such poor shape you'll end up wishing you'd never tried to use it. Whenever possible, make a first-hand assessment of this equipment before you put it to use.

Another approach for capturing and feeding back conversations is to use a computer connected to a projector, along with your choice of document-editing software. Simply type up words and ideas on behalf of others, while providing visual feedback on the shared screen. The digital document also creates a record of the capture that's quickly and easily shared and built on in later sessions. If you use collaborative software, you can also involve others in the capture, making the activity even more interactive.

STEP 3: CAPTURE WELL

Capturing well involves reflecting back the core ideas being discussed while keeping a close eye on digressions, just in case they develop into something important. A key challenge of this process is remaining attentive, perhaps even responding and asking for clarifications as you participate, while at the same time thinking about what you're hearing and the best way of summarising and refining it. In essence, you have to multitask. For this reason, if the resources allow it, I assign this job to an experienced professional.

If you do engage someone for this task, they should have the ability to understand the subject matter and translate the ideas into pithy summaries, diagrammatic overviews and pictorial representations. Increasingly, this role is known as *graphic scribing*, and the best in this field are highly sought after for their ability to maximise both the quality of the conversation in the moment, and the visual representation of what is said for future consideration or to be communicated to those unable to attend.

If you're doing the capture yourself, don't be afraid to pause the conversation for a moment to confirm your understanding of what's being said. In my experience, this won't significantly disrupt the discussion; rather, it gives people a minute to consider the words being spoken and to listen more deeply. Feeding back what you think you heard in your own words is also a powerful way to clarify your own understanding and that of the speaker –even if you're not confident that you have it right. It demonstrates that you're really listening and value the contribution being made, if not prompting a speaker to reflect on what they were trying to express.

Another part of capturing well is presentation. Making the words of your participants *look* good is a simple way of helping them feel confident and positive about their contributions, and thus the collaborative experience. So if you're going to be doing a fair bit of scribing for a session, take a few minutes beforehand to practise your writing style. For example, decide when you're going to use lower-case versus upper-case letters, how you'll represent headings versus sub-points, and when different colours will be used. Also test each marker to see if they all work, and make sure you have an eraser handy!

Practice and deep listening are the keys to great capture. With regular practice, you gain the ability to not only create strong representations of participant contributions, but to improve them. This occurs through a process I call *distilling* – finding a few key words or a phrase that captures the essence of what someone has said. In Collabforge workshops, our goal is to hear participants say, 'You captured what I said, but much more clearly than how I said it!'

Tool 16: Aligned Understandings

As discussed in Chapter 4, when you first bring people together to explore a collaborative proposition, there is the danger of 'ironing in wrinkles'. Social discomfort and a poverty of time can combine to push the participants into rushing their early discussions. When this happens, they take for granted simple terms, concepts and methods specific to the subject matter, and which are being used to ground the conversation. The risk here is that participants might use the same term but mean different things, and as a result, they end up agreeing to things they didn't mean to confirm. For example, I might say, 'Are we agreed that we need to collaborate closely to make this project work?' and you might reply, 'Yes of course!', only for both of us to find out that we each have a very different understanding of what it means to 'collaborate closely'. The use of Tool 15: Ideas on Display to externalise key concepts and ideas will significantly reduce the likelihood of ironing in these types of wrinkles. However, in your first meetings, it's worth going a little further.

STEP 1: IDENTIFY CORE TERMS AND CONCEPTS

As you enter your first conversations, take note of the terms and concepts that are being used by the group, especially those that are unique to the particular context or subject matter. Then, at an appropriate point of the discussion, introduce the notion of confirming the group's 'first principles' in order to quickly check that everyone is on the same page regarding the core ideas. Pick something that you feel is central to your initiative and ask your participants, 'What does this mean to you and why is it important?' It might be a broad concept, like 'a national social policy framework', or it might be a method, such as 'action research' or 'Agile project management'. Asking the participants to define and reflect on common concepts in their own words will help the group sense where there is shared understanding and where gaps or 'wrinkles' might exist.

STEP 2: DISCUSS AND PRIORITISE

Once you've addressed a starting concept or term with the group, pause the discussion and invite the participants to identify others, although have them hold off on providing definitions. Now write these up in a shared space, such as on a whiteboard or a projected screen. Once you've received a suggestion or two from each participant, ask the group to nominate which of these they feel it's crucial for everyone to understand in the same way, for the success of the collaboration.

As people make their nominations, put ticks next to them to represent their votes, creating a prioritised list that you can use to continue the discussion. In addition to focusing the conversation, this list also contributes to the group's shared understanding of what's important to all involved.

STEP 3: DEFINE AND SHARE

As the final step, define the top three terms or concepts as a group, at the same time capturing the definitions you all land on. Feel free to tackle more terms/concepts if you have time; if there are differing perspectives, just note them for later. If you plan to grow your group, these definitions will give you a strong starting point for bringing in new participants, minimising the chances of ironing in any wrinkles.

Tool 17: The LEGO Challenge

I often liken a group's first attempts at cocreation to the members of that group all trying to ride for the first time a bicycle made for [insert the number of participants here!]. Imagine a dozen people jumping onto a 12-seat bicycle and attempting to pedal it down the street. Things will be more than a little shaky until all those involved gain the confidence, experience and skill necessary to work together as a group. The fact that cocreation takes practice as a group is central to the third principle of collaboration: shared capability. This capability can only be built by individuals working together.

This tool was developed to provide a low-risk means of test-riding a new 'collaborative bike'. In fact, it was devised years ago with the assistance of my then 10-year-old twins as part of a school holiday program we run at Collabforge. The boys decided they wanted to create a collaboration program for kids, something that would be fast, easy and fun. The end result was The LEGO Challenge,[4] which was quickly adopted by my team at Collabforge for internal prototyping. It was an immediate hit when we began trying it in client workshops, and we've since run this challenge with groups as small as three and multi-team groups as large as 100. We've used it with senior executives, designers, developers and project managers. It never fails because it's a mixture of fun and a great opportunity to refine and prototype a group's ideas.

---

4 While it uses a significantly different process, The LEGO Challenge was informed by LEGO's own Serious Play method, which is more focused on individual problem-solving.

Developing a first-up rough-and-ready prototype is an extremely valuable way of helping a group to 'see what they think' as they move beyond discussion to being productive; it's doubly important for groups that are at the cold-start stage. A LEGO prototype gives a group something to react to that's meaningful and at the same time non-threatening.

STEP 1: PLAN

Each of the following steps should be timed to prevent them from going on too long. Typically, in time-constrained workshops, Collabforge makes each step seven minutes long. This sense of urgency moves the process along and keep the participants engaged. It also mirrors the fact that we never seem to have enough time for our collaborative projects!

For this first timed round, the group isn't allowed to touch the LEGO pieces (this happens in step 2). Instead, the idea is that the participants simply *discuss* what they're going to build to represent their collaborative aims. Prompts that you can provide on a slide, handout or just verbally include the following:

- What interactions will be required between people to generate the outcomes we want?
- What might these interactions look like?
- How might these outcomes generate impact and value?
- What will we build first?

Make sure you take some time to clarify the instructions before starting the timer for this step. Some people may need a little support to understand the idea that you're asking them to model some aspect of their collaboration in LEGO, otherwise it can feel somewhat abstract. Help them understand that the goal is not to talk about how to make a perfect LEGO model, but to discuss what the most important aspects of the collaboration will be. With these aspects in mind, once the building begins in step 2, the process tends to drive itself.

STEP 2: BUILD

As a general guide, a small-to-medium-size bowl of LEGO blocks works well for a group of six. Participants will find diverse and ingenious ways of encoding bricks with all kinds of meaning – I've seen a single green brick become the centrepiece of an entire creation! Also include some figures (LEGO characters, ideally one or more per participant) to prompt the consideration of human interactions and experience.

As soon as the timer has gone off at the start of this step, instruct the group to begin building. By all means encourage the participants to continue talking and planning, but remind them that they only have seven minutes to build something. Also make sure that the LEGO is accessible to everyone, as opposed to one or two individuals monopolising the bowl.

After having given a 'One minute left!' warning, I typically count down the final 10 seconds of the allotted seven minutes, to energise people to get the last of their pieces into place. That said, a couple of times I've seen the opposite happening, with the energy and excitement of these last seconds leading to the accidental destruction of the entire creation! Regardless, no matter what happens, stop the group when the timer goes off. I often exclaim 'LEGO down!' to stop the building, while also getting a few laughs.

STEP 3: REFLECT

Like step 1, step 3 is discussion-driven, but this time the participants must reflect on their planning and building experiences, both from an individual perspective and how they all went as a group. Here are some good prompts to use:

- How did you personally respond to this collaborative challenge? What did you do?
- Could you have responded in a way that would've provided more benefits to the group?

- Was there a moment when your group began working better or worse? Why did this happen?
- Does your model reflect your plan? What got built well? What didn't get built?

Going through the process of planning, building, then reflecting creates a microcosm of a collaborative project, from which many things can be learned about oneself, the group and the process. In particular, by providing a context where the outcome is de-risked by using materials that force participants to become more abstract, even playful, you allow them to be less guarded and more open.

The LEGO Challenge also exposes our collaborative muscle memory – how we unconsciously and automatically respond in a collaborative situation. Did a person sit back and watch others, waiting for the perfect moment to contribute? Or did they take a leadership role, helping others to cut through the indecision? Perhaps they started by organising all the materials with the aim of helping others get what they needed as fast as possible (this seems to be my default LEGO Challenge response). Sharing these reflections allows participants to focus on their individual innate collaborative strengths and weaknesses, as well as helping the group to understand the parts that will make up its whole as it begins to collaborate.

A Note on Trust

Beyond helping you understand your own collaborative muscle memory, Tool 17: The LEGO Challenge also builds trust among your participants. As they share their understandings and perspectives, they demonstrate to each another the knowledge and experience they have which are relevant to the collaborative proposition. This is the trust that comes when a participant asks themselves, 'Do these other people have the smarts or experience to help?' and answers in the affirmative.

Competence, however, is only one dimension of trust. Benevolence, or the degree to which we feel that someone will look after our best interests, irrespective of competence, is another.[5] Building up this dimension of trust requires more-personal and informal interactions, such as people having lunch together. At Collabforge, we've sought to create methods of trust-building that reinforce the understanding of both competency and benevolence, and in our experience, The LEGO Challenge does just that.

Tool 18: A Shared Definition of Collaboration

Tool 17 sets up a group perfectly to discuss the expectations they have for collaboration and what they think will be needed for it to succeed. Sometimes, individuals can get very uncomfortable talking about their roles in a collaboration, explaining how they'll contribute and the dynamics they expect this to create. A light-hearted experience like The LEGO Challenge helps to break the ice and defeat the self-consciousness that can otherwise impede progress.

This next tool lets your group deepen their reflections and capture the outcomes. The aim is to create a shared view regarding what collaboration could and should mean for your situation, which in turn moves your group closer to shared capability in collaboration.

STEP 1: REFLECT ON YOUR KEY COLLABORATION PRINCIPLES

Before running this activity with participants, consider the aspects of collaboration that are most important to you for your particular

5 The idea that competence and benevolence are both central to the building of trust originated in research on organisational leadership (see Kenexa High Performance Institute, *Trust Matters: New Links to Employee Retention and Well-Being*, 2011, http://www.mas.org.uk/uploads/artlib/khpi-work-trends-report-trust-matters.pdf) and was later applied to teamwork (IBM Software, *How Trust Optimizes Performance: the Mediating Role of Risk-Taking Behavior*, 2014, https://www.ibm.com/downloads/cas/XWLZOVMZ).

scenario. They might be those you feel are most needed to achieve the outcome; for example, transparency or collective decision-making. They might also be oriented towards the experience you want to have – 'learning oriented', or just 'fun and relaxed'.

STEP 2: ASK PARTICIPANTS WHY COLLABORATION IS IMPORTANT

This step is essentially the same as step 1, but it's done with your group. To begin with, ask the participants what collaboration means to them and what they think is important for success. I'd recommend a turn-taking approach for this discussion, preceded by some silent thinking and writing that gives people a minute or two to jot down their ideas. At Collabforge, we've found that this is a great way of priming conversations, as it allows people to compose their thoughts before sharing. We've also found that some people prefer to reflect *before* talking, while others prefer to think *by* talking – this process works for all concerned.

After the silent thinking and writing, share with the other members of the group what's personally important to you (the ideas you captured in step 1). This approach is based on a principle known as *first-mover dynamics* – the first mover in a conversation establishes a frame of reference for those who follow them, often without the subsequent speakers realising this. You can use the first-mover dynamic strategically, depending on the objectives of the conversation. If you're looking for fresh thinking that challenges your own, it's best to not start first. But if you want to provide specific framing, or guidance regarding a topic that may be new or challenging to participants, then go first.

STEP 3: LISTEN TO WHAT PARTICIPANTS SAY ABOUT COLLABORATION AND HOW THEY SAY IT

After the participants each have had a chance to share their views, you can move into free-flowing conversation. As the discussion opens up, do your best to capture the key points, ideally on a shared space such as a whiteboard.

It's important that you actively listen to what people are saying about collaboration and how they are saying it. Listen out for the emotions and intensity that do or don't come through. An individual's responses will be coloured by their past experiences as much as by their thoughts on the current experience. This can tell you a lot about how they'll react once the collaboration gets underway, as well as the expectations and assumptions they hold about what collaboration is and why it is or isn't important to them.

As you listen, also try to make connections with the points made in previous activities: specifically, Tool 17: The LEGO Challenge, Tool 16: Aligned Understandings and Tool 14: The Why–How–What Discussion. Look for anything that will deepen the conversation and link the ideas being shared to the proposed project. To push this along, you might ask the group to reflect on the 'How' part of Tool 14, which should describe how collaboration will happen. Do their views align with this, or is there more work to be done here? You might also ask if the perspectives shared on collaboration reflect the experience of The LEGO Challenge, or if there are specific gaps in capability that may need to be bridged.

Try to conclude with a handful of points, principles even, concerning what people agree is important going forward. If you can, try to capture these on a whiteboard or butcher's paper so that they're visible for the rest of the session. That means you won't necessarily need to refer to them directly – participants will see and occasionally reflect on them, and likely reference them in conversation. In fact, this is the goal. If participants pick up on and reference these points and principles, it means they're organically establishing their collaboration norms and principles, which is arguably the only way this happens effectively.

Tool 19: The Collaboration Plan

You might have noticed that the sequencing of tools in Part II takes progressively deeper and more collaborative passes at the same territory. For example, the value proposition for collaboration gets a first pass in Tool 1, which is focused on your own value proposition, and then again in Tool 9, which introduces the value proposed for others.

This iterative approach mirrors how collaboration happens in the real world: all facets of a collaboration continuously evolve in concert with one another. As a collaboration progresses, aspects change that impact other aspects; for example, when a new participant joins, it changes the vision for what's possible, which in turn may impact the methods for delivery, or the potential to involve others. Because of these interdependencies, any approach to designing and delivering collaboration must not only allow for this continual redefinition, it must make a virtue of it. The moments that signify the progression of a collaboration also represent an opportunity to realign and improve its plan and premise.

Tool 19 does this by building on the initial plan you created as part of Tool 6: A Draft Collaboration Design, and Tool 7: The Why–How–What Pitch. This time around, you'll incorporate the input of others, while also thinking about your group's strategic intent and how it can be supported by specific activities and planning.

STEP 1: CREATE A STRAWHORSE VOA STRATEGY

First you will create a strawhorse vision, outcomes and activities (VOA) strategy for your initiative using a simple yet effective format. It will tighten the focus even more from where Tool 7: The Why–How–What Pitch left off. Just like The Why–How–What Pitch , this tool comprises three elements that move from higher to lower levels of focus – from 'vision' to 'outcomes' and finally 'activities' (see Figure 6). Working from the top down, you can ask, 'How will our vision be realised by the specific outcomes, and what activities will be needed to produce those outcomes?' However, these elements work in the other direction as well. Working from the bottom up, you can ask, 'What activities will generate the outcomes we need to realise our vision?' Making sure your strategy works in both directions is a powerful means of sense-checking any ideas you have relating to any of the three areas.

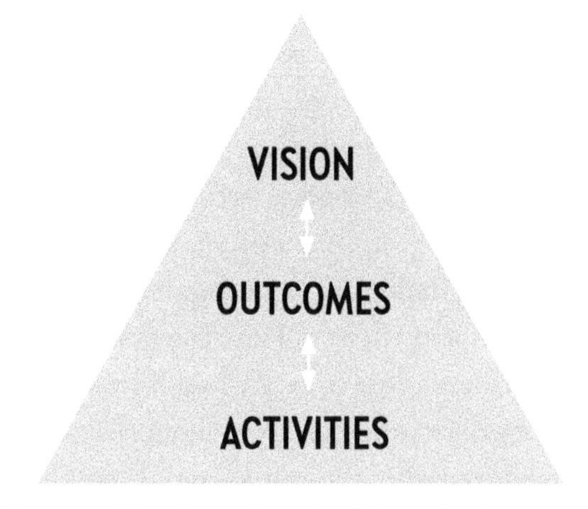

Figure 6. The Three Levels of the VOA Strategy

To create your strawhorse strategy, use your Draft Collaboration Design and Why–How–What Pitch as inputs and apply a dot-point level of detail under each of the VOA headings, in any order that makes sense to you. Do this individually (you'll involve the group in step 2) and don't get too caught up in defining your vision at this point. You can use the one you created as part of Tool 6: A Draft Collaboration Design. A short, pithy vision that everyone agrees with can take many conversations and many months to land on, and even then, for many projects its utility can be questionable. If you don't like the one you came up with previously, or you want to let the group help to define it from scratch, just leave this part of the strategy blank and prioritise 'outcomes' and 'activities' instead.

STEP 2: SHARE AND BUILD OUT YOUR STRATEGY WITH PARTICIPANTS

When you show the group your VOA strategy, be conscious of positioning it as a strawhorse: an early version that you want them to pull apart, even set on fire, but then help you to rebuild. Begin step 2 by asking the participants to do several minutes of silent writing focused on generating additions, changes or ideas for any level of the strategy, but stress that they should prioritise outcomes. Ideally, this writing should be done on sticky notes that can be added to the single version that the group will collectively create in the next step. Tell the participants to limit their ideas to one per sticky note, but encourage them to create as many sticky notes as they have ideas.

After several minutes of silent writing, ask someone to share what they feel is their most important outcome, and to pass you their sticky note on this while speaking to it. Place the note on a whiteboard or wall indicating its level; that is, in the middle for 'outcomes', higher for 'vision' and lower for 'activities'. Now ask for someone else to share a point that relates to what was just shared. If no-one has anything to contribute, ask for a point that is a contrast to the previous one, or from a different level of the strategy. Repeat this until you've collected and heard about all the sticky notes produced.

As you move through this process, try not to spend too much time wordsmithing or getting drawn into deeper discussion. Just concentrate on creating a shared representation of the group's contributions, organised according to the three-part VOA structure. And remember, as per step 1, don't get hung up on 'vision'. Make 'outcomes' the priority wherever possible. This will enable your group to more easily build up or down, starting from the centre.

STEP 3: CREATE A DRAFT WORK PLAN, COLLABORATIVELY

The draft strategy created in step 2 will be a valuable input for you and your group going forward. But for now, you'll use it to work towards a second goal: creating enough shared understanding, agreement and alignment to have a first crack at a work plan. Getting a feel for what work will need to be done, by whom and when, is an effective way of getting participants to understand the commitment required. It also kickstarts their productivity should they decide to get involved.

This step has you create a linear timeline that organises all the tasks, activities and deliverables that can contribute to the realisation of the VOA strategy. You'll need plenty of space for this, so you'll probably have to move from the whiteboard on which you captured your VOA to something larger and more accessible, like a tabletop or wall. In this space, define the beginning and end of your timeline by writing months, years or more-specific dates on pieces of paper and tacking them up.

Begin with a discussion of what the overall timeline should be. When can you start? What time-related impacts might there be, including holidays, financial planning and competing priorities? Does the project have a clear finish date or timeframe? If so, what is it, and are there any activities or aspects that will continue beyond this? If the initiative doesn't have a firm completion date, how far into the future can everyone imagine it going?

After establishing the timeline, ask participants to take the sticky notes from the 'activities' section of the VOA and organise them under these dates. Now do a second round of sticky-note brainstorming that fleshes things out further. Add secondary tasks that are necessary to complete the activities already listed. Also add the specific deliverables or objects that may result from these activities, but that are on a level below 'outcomes' on the VOA.

This can be a fairly free-flowing and discussion-driven activity, with everyone creating sticky notes and adding them as they're created. But watch out for cross-impacts or interdependencies; for example, an activity on the timeline that's out of sequence in regards to other, dependent activities. Whenever necessary, ask questions about the sequencing, as well as the purpose of any activities you don't understand. Finish by focusing on the near term: What needs to happen first, then second? What happens in the first three months?

A few years ago, I used this tool with a group of about 40 people representing 12 different government agencies, ranging from transportation, land management and social services, through to the Department of Premier and Cabinet (the peak agency for Australian state government). The participants had been charged with collaborating across all their organisations to strategically manage the ongoing development of a substantial section of a metropolitan city over the next 20 years. Thirty minutes and hundreds of sticky notes later, the group had created a wall plan that was about 2 metres high and some 5 metres long.

Given the scale of the collaborative challenge these people faced, it wasn't surprising that their plan would be so large and detailed. But the point is that prior to this activity, the members of each agency involved hadn't yet seen or understood the detail of the other agencies' perspectives and interests. When this happened, the group suddenly realised that there were all kinds of cross-impacts, and they were able to tease out specific expectations and interests held by different members but which previously had been unknown to the whole. Most importantly, this process prompted the key decision-makers to understand that there were serious issues with the plan that could threaten the entire collaboration. And it was clear that if these issues weren't dealt with immediately, the first year's worth of work would likely be in vain.

Tool 20: Detailed Participation Map and Core Formation

Now that Tool 19: The Collaboration Plan has provided a sense of the work to be done, and why it needs to be carried out, you can turn your attention to who should do this work. As per the second principle of collaboration – shared process – collaborative work falls into three categories: cocreation, cooperation and coordination (the 3Cs). In conjunction with the thinking done as part of Tool 8: Participant Mapping for the Core, Community and Crowd, we can use the 3Cs to assess the pointy end of it all: who is going to commit to regularly getting together and do the work of delivering the collaboration's outcomes.

STEP 1: PREPARE FOR PARTICIPANT MAPPING

To prepare for this activity, revisit your draft participant list from Tool 8 to see if your initial thinking still holds up. If you feel you now have a better understanding of your needs and/or interests regarding participants, take some time to refine this list.

To effectively involve the rest of your group in this process, you'll need to introduce the concepts that support it – specifically, the 3Cs. I've found that this can be done quickly and easily, and that it almost always prompts an immediate, deeper appreciation of the collaborative challenges and opportunities at hand. To provide a basic introduction to the 3Cs, simply draw the 'onion' diagram from Tool 8 (see Figure 5) on a whiteboard and describe each of its three layers. You can also find slides and other communication resources at Collabforge.com/collaboration-design.

STEP 2: UNDERTAKE COLLABORATIVE PARTICIPANT MAPPING

As you introduce the 3Cs mapping technique, demonstrate the concepts by showing where you feel those in the room might fit in. You might well be unsure about this, due to uncertainty over the group members' abilities or interest in committing, or the relevance of their expertise to activities at different stages in the project, but you can ask them for their thoughts on the matter. Try to get them to see and position themselves in the circles.

When asking participants to place themselves in the diagram, don't dwell too long on the finer points. Instead, consider this a means of reinforcing the participants' understanding of the 3Cs, and move as quickly as possible to a collective brainstorming session on who is not in the room but should be considered for inclusion. Use your previously prepared material to keep the conversation rolling along.

As you talk through potential participants, ask questions like:

1. What types of things will be produced by the cocreating core, and who will do it?
2. What types of cooperative, transactional exchanges will take place in the cooperating community?
3. Who are the decision-makers and financial controllers, and where do they fit in? What will their participation look like?
4. What individuals, groups and organisations need to be brought along on the journey as part of the coordinated crowd, and why? How will we reach them?

For larger groups, consider starting with silent sticky-note writing, with the notes then passed up to a whiteboard or wall. As discussed earlier, this helps maintain an equal weighting of the voices in the room and gives everyone time to think about their contributions. For smaller groups (six people or less), it's usually fine to run this activity as an organic discussion. Just ensure that you or someone else captures the suggestions in a way that simultaneously presents the content back to the group; for example, on a whiteboard, projected screen or the like.

STEP 3: DEFINE THE CORE

One of the surest indicators of collaborative success is how frequently a core group meets to do real work together. It's tempting for collaborative groups to try to organise their get-togethers and efforts in an ad-hoc way, assuming that they'll meet on an as-needed basis. But while this approach can be effective as a means of avoiding unnecessary meetings in more cooperative contexts, it will fall short in providing the time and interaction required to build shared capability for cocreation.

Your collaborative capability, and everything that supports it, flows from a regular rhythm of working together. Since your core group is the engine of your collaboration, it's essential that the basis of this regular participation is realistic. One of the biggest risks will be that this engine stalls just as you're getting moving.

To set realistic expectations, after you've completed a first pass at all three participant categories as part of step 2, return to the list created for the core. Discuss with your participants the following questions and, as always, capture the responses in a shared space to encourage reflection throughout the conversation. Also keep a clear record of all the people listed for all three categories, as you'll come back to this later.

1 Have we listed the right people in the core, individuals who'll be ready, able and available to get real work done? (It can be tempting to aspire to get senior decision-makers or influencers deeply involved, but while this has its merits, it doesn't always work well. Those in leadership positions are often used to providing feedback or decision-making input, not necessarily rolling up their sleeves and creating content. Decision-makers are often best placed in the cooperation list.)
2 What should the core's regular rhythm be, and how realistic is it that the team outlined can commit to this schedule? (Consider and discuss specific schedules, such as 'every other Tuesday, 10:00am – 12:00pm'.)
3 What will the core need to create first, and are there any dependent tasks or decisions? Will the right people be in the room and will they have the information they need?
4 Will the core need specific tools or software for managing their information, documents and communication? What would the likely default option be if the group simply used

what they've used before or are familiar with, and will this be appropriate for our needs? (For larger or more-complex projects, consider running the activity in Tool 4: The Shared Capability Baseline. Simply ask the questions in each step and ask the group to give a score. However, the score you get is less important than the conversation that happens as you go through this process.)

Your core group should aspire to mirror the types of routines, shared practices and norms found in tight-knit music groups and sporting teams. To achieve this, beyond establishing a regular rhythm of meeting, look for opportunities for informal interaction – members having lunch or dinner together is a good way to start. You all need to learn a little more about each other, to better understand your individual perspectives and motivations. The goodwill this creates will carry you through the tensions that will inevitably arise during the fourth stage of collaboration, which I discuss in the next chapter.

CHAPTER 10

Resolve

The third principle of collaboration, shared capability, tells us that resolving tension is a key capability that every group must build progressively as the members work together. In fact, resolving tension is perhaps the central function of, and value proposition for, collaboration. The resolution of collaborative tension is a generative force that has many forms: it can represent a problem solved or a solution found, a breakthrough made or a friendship forged. This is how collaboration *creates* and why it's so effective as a strategy.

This perspective involves a new way of interpreting our interactions with each other: as a result of coming together for a shared purpose, we generate tensions that provide the raw material for cocreation. As this dissonance, or lack of harmony, among participants is resolved into consonance, it transforms into shared value – newly created through the efforts of those involved. So tension and dissonance should be expected and welcomed. This can even mean explicitly seeking tensions that may be lurking under the surface, as yet unexpressed.

But don't take this as an excuse to argue for the sake of argument. A fight can be satisfying, but it's rarely productive when collaborating. And beware of the tendency we all have to fight for the ideas in which we're personally invested, even when they're not the best ones. In essence, make sure you're fighting for the best result, not just to win.

It takes lots of practice to recognise a moment of collaborative dissonance and put your own emotions and interests aside long enough to see the best solution available to your group. I still struggle with this myself, even after more than a decade of pretty much daily, conscious collaborative practice. The trick is that, as you resolve collaborative dissonance, you have to be careful not to subjugate your own needs, interests and beliefs in the process. You have to strike a balance between the interests of the group and those of its members (including yourself). It's precisely this that shifts a collaborative outcome from groupthink to 'more than the sum of its parts'.

Within this chapter, you'll find a range of tools for resolving tension. At Collabforge, we've used these tools in many different contexts, with consistent success. Keep in mind, however, that a tool is only as good as the hand that wields it. Expect a little practice in order to become proficient. Above all, deploying these tools effectively requires that you maintain a state of active listening, reflection and goodwill.

Very early in the life of Collabforge, I experienced first-hand what happens when tension isn't effectively resolved and boils over. In that instance, a group of small-business owners working to cocreate a government program became confused and annoyed by a particular process. Due to my inability at the time to *hear* this coming from them, as well as not having well-tested methods for surfacing and resolving tension, a subset of the group hijacked the workshop and revolted! Needless to say, our government client wasn't very happy. This uncomfortable experience prompted me to work even harder on how to support groups to communicate and resolve their tensions. Fast-forward nearly a decade: Collabforge has developed many tools for this purpose, and the norm now is for the groups we work with to regularly have tension-resolving breakthroughs.

As an example, when we were commissioned by a metropolitan transportation agency, we worked with community members and tech experts to develop a *hackathon*, a process that incentivises participants to develop software solutions for a particular problem. The transport agency had lots of newly available live data, but not the innovation capability to figure out how to best make use of it. As our group came together, significant tensions emerged around the best formats for releasing this live data. They were fuelled by the ideological differences among the participants – some advocated for more-proprietary approaches, while others were firmly in the open-access and open-source camps of software development.

Collabforge's methods, including our focus on recognising the needs and interests of those involved, meant we could support the group to overcome these differences and find approaches that were acceptable to everyone. The resulting hackathon process was strongly supported by the wider tech and start-up community and generated 13 market-ready apps, well beyond our initial goal of three apps.

Unlike the tools in the other chapters, those presented here are less likely to be deployed sequentially in one or more sessions. Instead, you should consider the nature of the tensions you've encountered and use these tools selectively. To help you figure this out, in the introduction to each tool you'll find a *Use this tool* sub-section, with recommendations as to which situations they're most applicable to.

The first two tools surface tension by providing a means for individuals to jump straight to what they believe is the most important thing, removing the need to provide a justification or rationale. Tool 23, on the other hand, is a constructive process for sharing emotional states, using the insights gained to inform the group's priorities. Tool 24 applies a more-traditional feedback process to surface tensions, and offers several methods for helping your group understand what to do with the feedback generated.

Sometimes, significant tensions can be experienced when a group is creating or making sense of complex subject matter. Tool 25 helps the participants to collectively draw out, break down and organise this complexity. If you feel that your group generally is struggling to raise and resolve tensions, have a look at Tool 26, which sets out a diagnostic process for assessing your group's overall collaboration capability. The final tool provides a means for exploring the tensions of key stakeholders who, for whatever reason, you are not able to directly involve.

Tool 21: Question-Storming

Simply surfacing tension can be very challenging. Most people find it difficult to share views or opinions that are critical of the approaches or ideas of those whom they like and respect. But just because these views aren't shared doesn't mean they disappear. Rather, they can fester, leading to bigger problems down the track – in some cases, unresolvable problems. It's far better to address them in the early stages of a collaboration, while they're still relatively minor and more easily managed.

In fact, merely surfacing tensions can do a lot of the work needed to resolve them. Often, when participants are aligned with the same goal, they naturally seek a resolution when difficulties are raised. This is especially true if the tensions are presented constructively and in a non-personal manner. Remember that resolving tension builds trust, as well as delivering shared value. So don't shy away from it!

This tool provides the simplest means I've yet encountered for productively surfacing tensions. The use of questions to reveal issues or concerns is highly constructive because questions, at least in theory, have answers. This approach also pushes participants to think through and consolidate their ideas before sharing them.

Another key to this activity's effectiveness is that doesn't seek to answer the questions on the spot. Rather, it focuses on airing them – you can deal with them later when there's more context, time and focus to do so, with the full understanding of the participants that they'll be addressed in due course.

Use this tool at the outset of any collaboration, or alternatively when you feel that people have unspoken questions or issues that are preventing them from being fully present or involved. You can also use it when you feel that participants are unsure as to the value or purpose of a meeting, workshop or work session.

STEP 1: PREPARE FOR AND INTRODUCE THE ACTIVITY

Make sure you have some clear space on a whiteboard, butcher's paper, or a projected document that's open and ready: you'll need to capture the questions as quickly as they're spoken. Ideally, your question-capture space will be accessible throughout your session. You want to be able to return to the questions whenever necessary to add to them, point to them if they come up again, and note when they've been addressed.

When introducing the activity, make it clear that the goal is to reveal and capture all questions regarding the day and/or the initiative, but *not* to answer them right now – they'll be considered in depth at a later stage. Right now, their purpose is to inform the flow of the day, helping the facilitators to make decisions about prioritising content, and to understand what the participants interests' and issues are. Welcome and capture all questions, even if they feel off-topic.

STEP 2: SOLICIT QUESTIONS AND PROBE

To begin the activity, use a focus question like 'What questions do you have about this initiative?' or 'What questions would you like to have answered by the end of our session today?' It may take a little time to get things started, so be careful not to cut short the time needed for someone to raise the first point.

When a new group is first asked a question, rarely will there be an immediate response. The question will create an awkward space that most new participants are hesitant to step into. To deal with this, I like to use a technique I call the *pregnant pause*, which is when you remain patient and feign comfort while the gestation time or silence needed for someone to respond passes – this always seems to be exactly the amount of time it takes until you feel you can't possibly wait another second for someone to offer the first point! At your next opportunity, give this technique a try. Given enough time, someone will speak, I guarantee it, and once they do, others will jump in right after. If you have a particularly shy group, tell them you're using the pregnant pause technique and that you're going to wait for someone to speak. This lets them know that you're not going to move on until someone offers something.

Once the questions start coming, record them as quickly as possible, double-checking that you've written them down correctly before moving on to the next person. Remember, resist the temptation to answer them; if anyone else steps in to provide an answer, gently remind them that the goal is to identify the questions, with time allowed to actually address them later on.

To keep things moving quickly, I recommend having two people run this activity: one captures the questions, intent only on listening, translating and writing clearly, while the other fields questions and manages the interactions in the room. That second person can also look for any themes that link the questions, perhaps illustrating these by grouping questions under particular labels – this can be especially useful when it comes to larger groups, as it will help you to eventually address groups of questions, as opposed to having to answer them one by one.

STEP 3: REVIEW QUESTIONS AND MANAGE EXPECTATIONS

Once the questions have ebbed – this often happens near the 10-minute mark for groups of between 10 and 30 people – review the capture and then give everyone a final chance to add more questions. At this point, if there are any questions to which you can provide simple responses, then do so, without allowing yourself more than one minute per question (consider using your watch to enforce this). Knocking off a few questions can help participants feel more at ease and prompt them to participate more fully. But again, don't get drawn into any discussion or debate.

You can manage participant expectations regarding exactly how you're going to address all the questions by letting them know that you've put aside some time at the end of the session to see what has or hasn't been answered. Also, if your session plan allows for it, let them know you'll check in with the questions along the way; for example, just before or on return from a break. Take such opportunities to point out questions that seem to have been answered.

When you're finally ready to provide answers, it's a good idea to ask the participants which questions they feel are the most important to respond to. And don't feel that it's solely your responsibility to answer them. Ask the participants to provide answers if they can. Finally, if you run out of time to deal with all the questions, commit yourself to following them up – some questions will require further collaboration to clarify and resolve.

Tool 22: Hearts and Elephants

Tension often comes in the form of conflicting or unclear priorities. This tool provides an effective way of surfacing such tensions by focusing on individual interests and priorities. Groups typically optimise their efforts around what their members feel is important, once the collective knows what these things are. On the other hand, if an individual feels strongly about something and they believe it isn't being addressed, it can increase their own disappointment and limit their ability to participate fully.

Use this tool when a group is unclear about its priorities or has already spent a good deal of time thinking hard about the initiative and needs to begin planning the work. Hearts and Elephants also works well as an *unblocker*, helping a group decide how to best move forward in the face of complexity. Essentially, this tool will assist a group to find out what's most important to the members.

STEP 1: CREATE ONE HEART AND ONE ELEPHANT EACH

Explain the rationale for this activity to your participants. That is, each of them instinctively knows both the most important issue/s at hand and the top-of-mind issues that are the most concerning or are preventing the project from moving forward. This tool prompts each participant to focus on one *heart of the matter* for them at this moment, and one *elephant in the room* that hasn't received enough attention.

Someone might choose a heart because it's their favourite aspect of the project, or because it's the most significant opportunity or challenge they see. It may be high-level or very specific. There aren't any rules about what is and isn't valid. The same goes for elephants. An elephant may be chosen because someone feels the group just hasn't gotten around to talking about it yet, or it may be something they feel their peers are shying away from but which is important to address head-on. In fact, it may be something that they themselves have been shying away from, not having found the right moment to raise it yet – this type of elephant is, in fact, ideal.

After making these points, ask everyone to jot down one heart and one elephant, either on separate sticky notes or on their own notepads (these two approaches will be dealt with in step 2). When making this request, it can be helpful to narrow the scope of consideration. For example, you might ask for one heart and one elephant in the context of whatever your group is focused on at that time, be it short-term priorities, a strategy, or next year's financial planning.

STEP 2: SHARE YOUR HEARTS AND ELEPHANTS, INDIVIDUALLY

Give everyone a few minutes to write down their hearts and elephants in silence. There shouldn't be a discussion at this point. Rather, you want each person to consider and develop responses from their own perspective. Watch the room, and when most people start looking up, ask for someone to volunteer a heart – I always start with hearts so that the group begins to open up with the more-positive and less-confronting topics.

For smaller groups, consider writing the hearts and elephants on a whiteboard or something similarly prominent, as they are shared, to help the participants reflect on the contributions as they're made. For larger groups, sticky notes are helpful, as you can put them up on a wall (or whiteboard) and quickly move them into groups or clusters. As per step 2 of Tool 21: Question-Storming, you can collect contributions under themes to move beyond individual perspectives to a collective representation.

After the first heart has been contributed, using the same process as step 2 of Tool 19: The Collaboration Plan, ask if anyone has a heart or elephant that they feel is in some way related to it. This will keep the topics unfolding in a way that maintains some flow and continuity, while encouraging clusters of like-themed contributions. If no-one has a related point, then ask for something contrasting or totally different to shift gears.

Ask each participant to read out their contribution, and if necessary to provide more context or explanation. It's always a good idea for you to go first in these sorts of activities, not just to help put the others at ease but also to model how it should work. In this case, being succinct and straightforward is important. Try to only speak to the words on the sticky notes. A good guideline, for you and the other participants, is to devote about 60 seconds to each heart and elephant.

STEP 3: DISCUSS

Once the group has shared all of their hearts and elephants, move into an open conversation to explore any themes that have emerged. Allow about 10–30 minutes for this, depending on the size of your group and the importance or complexity of the subject matter. This can be an important discussion, where priorities can be identified or refocused. It also gets participants on the same page concerning what they value about the collaboration at that moment, in both positive and negative respects (opportunities and challenges). As I've stressed elsewhere in this book, a shared understanding is one of the most important ingredients for catalysing and maintaining great collaboration.

Tool 23: Check-in

Our emotions are often one step ahead of our reasoning. They can alert us to the challenges and opportunities that confront us personally but which we aren't yet able to verbalise *rationally.* That's why sharing emotions during a collaboration can help you to identify and iron out wrinkles, while also clearing your head for the rigours of participation. Importantly, it also gives group members a view into each others' internal worlds, helping them better understand and connect with one another.

This is not entirely straightforward, however. Engaging emotions in organisational or collaborative settings requires a safe space and a process that supports open sharing and vulnerability. It's also necessary to support others to interact with the feelings shared, so as not to have undue criticism or confrontation undermine the perspective of the one doing the sharing.

This tool was developed for these purposes by Jim and Michele McCarthy after a decade of working with teams to improve collaborative performance, originally at Microsoft and then as independent consultants; it was first published in their 2002 book *Software for Your Head.* Some aspects of the process may feel awkward at first, but it has been carefully optimised through thousands of iterations and has delivered great results every time I've used it.

Use this tool when there is tension present within your group but the source is either unclear or charged with emotion. This might occur ahead of the delivery of a major milestone, or after a planning session when participants are really feeling the crunch. Check-in also works wonderfully as a regular part of a monthly team catch-up or the like, helping participants to reconnect while building the benevolence side of trust.

STEP 1: INTRODUCE THE ACTIVITY

As this tool focuses on emotions, its introduction is important in helping participants feel comfortable enough to give it a try. Make it clear from the outset that the goal is to share emotional states regarding the task or initiative at hand, as a means of better understanding what the group feels is important. Also let everyone know that this isn't a process you've just made up, but rather one that has been used thousands of times over several decades by high-performing teams – at Microsoft, Collabforge and many other organisations. Remind them that no-one is to comment on or discuss the emotions shared, and that everything shared is valid. Finally, emphasise that if anyone doesn't feel up to participating, they have an unconditional out.

STEP 2: TAKE TURNS SHARING: ARE YOU SAD, GLAD, MAD OR AFRAID?

Frame the activity with an initial statement like, 'We're going to share how we feel about our collaboration and the work ahead of us'. Feel free to set whatever scope you think is appropriate. Don't shy away from linking Check-in to a specific goal or milestone that the group is feeling particularly anxious about. And mention that this activity is not to be recorded in notes of any kind.

Next, let the participants know that they're welcome to pass on their turn if they don't feel they have anything substantive to share, or if they don't feel comfortable doing so. However, to pass, they must be 'checked in' to the broader initiative; that is, they must be ready to work collaboratively and committed to contributing their best. If they aren't feeling checked in, then ask them politely but unconditionally to leave the room while others share their feelings – but invite them to return when they do feel checked in and are ready to participate fully in the collaboration.

In all my years of using this tool, I've never had anyone 'check out', but it's an important option to provide. Occasionally, participants will pass on their turn but maintain a positive commitment to the initiative. Again, this is an important option for folks to know they have.

Once the group is ready, outline the following check-in process. Do your best to courteously help participants to stick to it as a set of rules. People can forget or interject or disrupt the process without realising or meaning to.

1. Start with yourself – the person who calls for a check-in must go first. Share your feelings using only one of the four primary emotions: sad, glad, mad or afraid. Don't speak to any other emotions. For example, you might say, 'I feel *afraid* that I won't have the time to deliver my next critical task because I've been asked to take on a new role in addition to my current one, and I don't want to let the group down'. Don't, however, say, 'I feel *anxious* that ...'
2. After your turn, the other participants take it in turns to speak. No-one is to interrupt, comment, or start a discussion. This is to be strict individual turn-taking, with no other contributions allowed.
3. After each person has spoken, they must say 'I'm checked in' to signal the end their turn and that they've said all they wish to say. In response, the other participants must reply with, 'Welcome!' This last step can feel cheesy at first, but it's essential because it tells the person who has just shared that they've been heard and their emotions have been accepted. It also lets the next person know that they can proceed.

Don't be surprised if emotions overflow a little. On more than one occasion, I've unexpectedly been faced with executives in tears. Sometimes it's not the person sharing who gets overwhelmed but those who are listening. I remember one instance when a participant was feeling sad about their inability to be fully involved in a project because they were going through the very painful process of moving their mother into assisted-care housing. Others in the group were very moved by this, not having known what was going on behind the scenes.

If participants get unexpectedly emotional, just stick to the process and do your best to stay relaxed. I've never had a bad outcome from using this tool in a disciplined way, and I've used it many times in many different settings. I've always found that it works amazingly well, with the group feeling refreshed and considerably more connected afterwards.

STEP 3: DISCUSS THE EXPERIENCE

After everyone has had a chance to share their feelings, take some time to discuss the experience by asking the participants for their big takeaways, reflections and realisations. But first, it's important to ask them to avoid specifically referencing anyone else in their comments and instead discuss things more generally, as well as to refrain from capturing these observations (as per the contributions in step 2). This ensures a safe space in which participants will feel freer to share openly, and to trust one another afterwards.

Tool 24: Soliciting Constructive Feedback

Of all the possible sources of tension, one of the most common is a simple critique of an idea or approach. One person's well-meaning suggestion, question or contribution can lead to any number of collaborative tensions. Indeed, depending on how it's solicited, constructive criticism can be quite *deconstructive*. So it's essential to have reliable methods at hand for garnering feedback.

This tool helps you gather feedback constructively by soliciting reactions along four different lines: what participants really like about a concept, what they would change, what questions they have, and any ideas they have on doing things differently. These categories overlap a little, but their main purpose is to provide a space for different types of participants to think into.[6]

Use this tool if you need feedback from particular people but you think that they may not be comfortable freely sharing their thoughts. Also use it if you think you'll be receiving feedback that's more critical than constructive. In these cases, this tool will help depersonalise the conversation, dissociating the critical concepts from people by externalising them. This means participants can focus the conversation on ideas rather than on each other. This tool also works well when you simply want to test an idea or get some reactions. On a cautionary note, be aware that this process can trigger transactional, cooperative dynamics, whereby others will assume that you'll respond to and integrate all the feedback that's given – you may need to devote some time to managing expectations if this won't be the case.

STEP 1: PREPARE FOR CAPTURE AND INTRODUCE THE ACTIVITY

When introducing this tool, let the participants know that they'll be asked to provide feedback, but through four different lenses. While constructive criticism is one of these, you'll look at other ways of improving the concept under discussion. Now create four quadrants on a whiteboard or piece of butcher's paper, or in a shared digital space. Label each of the squares with one of the following: 'Love', 'Change', 'Ideas' or 'Questions'.

---

6 This tool was inspired by the 'Feedback Capture Grid Method' created by Stanford University's Hasso Plattner Institute of Design, also known as the d.school (visit https://dschool-old.stanford.edu/sandbox/groups/dstudio/wiki/2fced/attachments/1ba97/Feedback-Capture-Grid-Method.pdf?sessionID=a4c32167e58dc598ac57b770de7cb0f4f838ac50).

STEP 2: CAPTURE THE FEEDBACK

Begin the activity by asking if anyone has something they'd like to contribute. Be sure to wait comfortably and silently, providing a healthy pregnant pause so that they can think and formulate a response.

As participants begin giving their feedback, keep a mental note of who has and hasn't contributed. After most people have had a chance to contribute, ask those who haven't given feedback if they have any thoughts to share. Similarly, consider asking the group for thoughts regarding any quadrants that haven't received much input. The goal is to get a holistic picture of the feedback, to enable improvement of the concept under scrutiny.

STEP 3: DISCUSS THE IMPLICATIONS

Be aware that, as mentioned above, this process can lead to people expecting that you will do the work of addressing and integrating all the feedback. This may be completely appropriate for your setting – for instance, if you're engaging those in your cooperating community. But if you're running this process with your cocreating core, you risk producing an integration bottleneck, as discussed in Chapter 4. Not only will this create work for you that would ideally be distributed among your core group, it also risks setting up a pattern of others looking to you to do the bulk of the work and decision-making.

If working with your core group, to avoid this, end the activity with a discussion of what the feedback means or seems to be suggesting. Ask high-level questions like 'Will addressing this feedback be limited to small tweaks and refinements?', 'Does it suggest deeper flaws, with the concept needing a substantive overhaul?', and 'Does it suggest that there are gaps that need improvement but not wholesale redesign?'

Once the group is in agreement as to the implications of the feedback and the scale and scope of the work needed to address these, discuss who within the group is best placed to do this work. Some elements might be addressed by one person, while others might require input from the whole group. In regards to highly collaborative groups, it's important to remind the participants that opportunities to 'divide and conquer' are well worth looking for, to get through more work more quickly than would be done through collaboration. Lastly, discuss a timeline for integrating the feedback. By talking through all of these elements, you should be able to overcome any integration bottlenecks that might otherwise occur.

A Note on Whether to Persevere or Pivot

Over the last few years, much has been made of the notion to *persevere* or *pivot*. That is, as a result of what you've just learned, should you continue as planned, or chart a new course? This concept can be fittingly applied to collaborative projects due to the need to continuously assess a group's emerging outcomes and how these are or aren't validating the shared vision.

While the notion of whether to persevere or pivot seems fairly simple and intuitive, it's rarely easy to make the decision to depart from a well-established plan. The ability to ask the question 'Does this feedback suggest that we should pivot?' depersonalises what can otherwise be a difficult discussion for those who are deeply invested.

Tool 25: Brainstorm, Bundle and Bind - the 3Bs

Confronting complexity and information overload gives rise to its own type of tension, and this is a common issue for collaborative groups. One of the primary reasons for collaborating, after all, is to address an issue or develop a solution that is too complex for any one individual to handle. However, the more information, competing priorities and different perspectives that a group has to consider, the faster things can break down. Sometimes, even the sheer volume of creative ideas can overload a group.

Regardless of its source, this type of tension often manifests as an inability of the group to hold a shared understanding of a topic, or to see a strategic pathway that leads through it all. This increases stress and contributes to a feeling of being overwhelmed. Comprehension may also be unevenly distributed, with some individuals having a better understanding than others – until the whole group has a solid collective understanding, the collaboration will likely remain stuck.

This tool, nicknamed *the 3Bs*, allows a group to quickly make sense of complexity; the subject matter can be anything, and the group doesn't need to do any preparation. Because the tool is so effective at collaboratively organising lots of information into an overall structured understanding, at Collabforge we often call it 'a framework for making frameworks'. It allows a group to see the shared understanding appear before them, while also building their shared ownership in its cocreation.

Use this tool when a group is holding or producing large amounts of information and the members need to rapidly make sense of it together. This need can arise from a project goal; for example, the development of a strategic approach by garnering lots of diverse inputs. It can also arise when a group becomes overwhelmed, with its ability to communicate and create a shared understanding and vision suffering as a result. This tool is therefore especially helpful when a group needs to arrive at a shared understanding of a complex domain or subject matter, but they have no ready-to-use frameworks.

STEP 1: BRAINSTORM ALL THE ELEMENTS, IDEAS AND ISSUES

Choose a focus statement, the scope of which should reflect your ambition. For example, if your group is just trying to decide the best way forward when a great many possibilities and ideas are being proposed, your statement might be, 'Brainstorm all of the ways in which we might address this challenge'. However, if your group is trying to build a shared understanding of a large subject-matter area, then the statement might be, 'Brainstorm all the elements, issues and ideas relating to [insert the subject-matter area]'.

Now set a timer for five minutes and ask folks to write down as many individual elements as can be clearly related in that timeframe – one element per sticky note. Depending on the size of your group and the complexity you face, you can consider breaking up the brainstorm into a few *sprints*. The first sprint might involve naming all the parts of the issue or area, the second might deal with ideas or issues, and so on. You don't need to focus on any particular rationale or logic at this stage. The goal is to obtain the greatest quantity of ideas: as many as possible within your timed sprint.

STEP 2: BUNDLE IT ALL INTO DIFFERENT GROUPINGS

After the timer goes off, have the participants speak to their sticky notes, posting them up on a wall or whiteboard as they do – or you can post them yourself (the larger the group, the more facilitation support will be required). In either case, the aim is to create clusters or thematic bundles.

Initially, just bundle the elements intuitively, clustering individual notes together in any way that seems to make sense. As bundles begin to take form, discuss with the group how they can be understood and what they should be called. Coming to a shared understanding of what the group is seeing is the most important outcome, over aspects like the language used for the bundles, which can be refined later. Finally, using a new sticky note or piece of paper, or by writing on a whiteboard if you're posting the notes to one, label each bundle.

STEP 3: BIND THE BUNDLES BY SEQUENCE OR PROCESS

Once all the bundles have been labelled, direct the discussion towards how they relate to one another. These relationships are typically characterised by either a process ('X bundle happens before Y bundle') or a specific logic ('X bundle is a feature of, or influences, Y bundle in a certain way'). Of course, there are other ways in which bundles can relate, and it's fine to use any rationale that makes sense. The important thing is that the relationships are discussed, agreed, named and labelled accordingly, which typically involves drawing lines that connect the bundles.

As you do this, reorganise and adjust the content to improve the visual appeal. This will be important to the group, partly because the more organised the content is, the better it will be understood. But you also want this to look like a valuable cocreation, one that the group is excited about and proud of. You want the participants to look at it and think, 'Wow, look at what we just produced. That looks amazing!' This is a key signal that you've just resolved tension and translated it into shared value, which is the goal of this tool – and collaboration in general.

After your session, consider creating a second graphical representation of the high-level aspects of your 3Bs framework, excluding some of the detail in the individual sticky notes. This consolidated representation is a powerful means of confirming the shared understanding that this activity has generated within the group. It allows the participants to move up a level in their thinking by letting go of the detail and focusing on the synthesis of their collective ideas.

Many times, I have seen the synthesised, high-level results of a 3Bs process become a central part of a collaboration's communication package, often going on to be refined throughout a project's lifetime. These representations can become key reference points for the group, helping to manage tension in the later stages of collaboration by revealing what is in or out of scope, or what is or isn't aligned with the group's strategic outlook. A cocreated reference point regarding scope and strategy is one of the most powerful complexity-cutting, tension-resolving tools a collaborative group can have.

Tool 26: A Collaboration Self-Assessment

As discussed briefly at the end of Tool 24: Soliciting Constructive Feedback, sometimes tension arises not so much from complexity but from a group's inability to identify, distribute and manage the work that needs to be done. Occasionally, you can point to an individual who is taking on less than their share of the work. But most of the time, it's actually more than one person who is creating the issue. Collaborative behaviours are shared by a group and are reinforced by what participants demonstrate to one another.

If you find that participants are consistently manoeuvring away from taking on work themselves, or are struggling to develop productive collaborative practices with one another, you may be experiencing a deeper issue that's prompting resistance to the development of a collaborative culture. This can happen for a number of reasons, which can be difficult to diagnose.

In Chapter 5, I explained the importance to individuals and groups of self-reflection, as a way of building the capability to collaborate more consciously. Beyond becoming more intentional in your collaboration, self-reflection is one of the best ways of increasing your productivity as a group: it's only by becoming self-aware of your deficiencies that you can learn when and how to correct them.

Use this tool when you feel that your group is underperforming, that for some reason it hasn't developed the collaborative capability you think it could or should have. It will help you zoom into the key dynamics of your collaboration and assess how well the participants are working, and if you need to intervene.

STEP 1: SELF-REFLECT ('SELF' MEANING YOU)

Step 1 is to be done by you individually. You may find that it gives you the answers and insights you need, negating the need for step 2. Perhaps these answers enable you to make some small, targeted interventions that help the group to meet a specific challenge, which may be more productive than focusing everyone's attention on 'serious' collaboration problems.

At other times, however, it can turn out that the problem is you. For most of us, our first response when we encounter social tension is to seek external causes – in other words, we struggle to see our own role in the issue, forgetting that we're all active participants in the collaborative dance. So it's important that you have a grounded understanding of what dynamics you're helping to create or reinforce.

Before answering the questions below, recall the last collaborative activity or group session you were involved in that didn't go as well as it could have. Close your eyes and try to remember who was in the room, how you felt, and why you felt that way. Was there food or drink? If so, what was it and how did it taste? This will help trigger more memories. Once you can adequately remember your state of mind and that of those who were there with you, respond to the following questions – the first three are multiple-choice, while the final question requires a descriptive answer.

Q1 Did you feel that you actively participated to help the group cultivate a shared understanding and shared vision?

A1 No / Some / Yes / Strongly

Q2 Did you 'lean in' to the activity, contributing ideas and positive energy while helping with the heavy lifting?

A2 No / Some / Yes / Strongly

Q3 Do you feel that your contributions improved the final outcome?

A3 No / Some / Yes / Strongly

Q4 What might you do differently next time to get more impact from your participation or to improve the group's performance?

A4 ______________________________

Reflect on your answers and consider how indicative they are of your overall role in that collaboration, beyond the specific activity or session that you recalled. Often they will be, so try to step back and objectively see yourself in this particular collaborative mix. How might others characterise your involvement? What might they have thought you were thinking during those moments of tension?

There are clearly no right or wrong answers to these types of questions – you'll probably never know what others thought. But formulating an opinion of yourself and the role you played is the first step in improving the outcome next time. The second is to remember this assessment in your next collaborative session and reflect on it in real time. Create a situation where you can consciously and purposively modify your behaviour to improve the dynamics, if not the outcomes. Try to action the answer you provided in question 4 above. Of course, you may not get the ideal result the first time around, but by continuing to test and learn, your capability – and your group's – will improve.

Genuinely reflecting during this activity can be challenging because it may bring up results and issues that you'd rather not have to confront. For example, I recently applied this tool to myself to better understand my role within a community collaboration, in particular a moment I experienced where significant tension emerged. While I wasn't directly involved – tempers flared between two people trying to cocreate content – I realised through the above process that I'd done nothing to help resolve the tension. At the time, I told myself I was staying out of the way so that the pair could build the capability to resolve tensions on their own. But on deeper reflection, I recognised that I was in fact unconsciously hoping that the collaboration would fail, to avoid the difficult job of being honest about my desire to leave the initiative. So before you apply this tool to your group, appreciate that difficult realisations may come up for those involved.

STEP 2: HAVE A GROUP REFLECTION (OPTIONAL)

In order to decide if you should run this step, consider your participants' likely reactions to being asked the questions you just answered.

As best as you can, think through the types of realisations they might have. Can you anticipate some of the background issues or troubles they may be experiencing? How do you think the questions will make them feel? As though they're being judged? Will they become defensive? Or will they be interested, even excited to develop their interpersonal skills? Different groups can react very differently, and as mentioned above, these reactions may not be conducive to improving your group's collaboration capability.

If you feel that the questions won't catalyse a significant negative response, or that even if they do, working through a negative response will be the best path forward, then run the same process you just went through. Ask the group members to recall the last less-than-ideal collaborative situation they experienced, as well as the associated smells, tastes and so on – I know it sounds goofy, but it really works in helping people to place themselves back in the situation. Now ask the participants to individually and privately write down answers to the four questions in step 1, after typing these questions into a slide and projecting them, or writing them up on a whiteboard.

Also add this fifth question:

Q5 Do you feel your answers are indicative of your overall participation in the collaboration, beyond this specific instance?

A5 No / Some / Yes / Strongly

Give everyone a few minutes in which to think and write – including yourself.

Even though you've already answered the questions (excluding the last one), consider them afresh by bringing to mind a different collaboration situation, to see if your answers still come out the same.

STEP 3: HAVE A GROUP DISCUSSION

For this tool's third and final step, there are several approaches you might take depending on the severity of your group's challenges, as well as their willingness and the time they have available to reflect on and engage with the issue.

The simplest option is to discuss the results of step 2. For this, I suggest that, rather than pushing people to openly share all their answers, instead take a softer tack. Start with a prompt question like, 'Does anyone have an answer to question 4 that they are comfortable sharing?' Allow a healthy pregnant pause, and then, when someone shares their answer, follow up with a request for that person's answer to question 5. At this point, don't comment on their contribution; just thank them for sharing and then ask if anyone else is willing to voice their answers to questions 4 and 5. As the group opens up, let the discussion flow more organically, and when it feels right, bring the participants to the question, 'Given what we've heard, what should we do to improve?'

Capture the results of this discussion on a whiteboard or other shared space, and finish the conversation by trying to be specific about how these changes can be made in your next working session.

A second, more-intensive approach, which follows on from the above, basically introduces more direct questions after the answers to questions 4 and 5 have been shared. These new questions should identify your collaboration challenges. They do not seek to solve the problems, however, as the best solutions tend to come from within a group, once the nature of the issue has been identified.

Questions that help to identify common collaboration challenges include the following (rephrase them as appropriate to pose them to your group):

1 Does your group use common, agreed definitions for central ideas and concepts? Or do you find that confusion arises

around the use of specific words, acronyms, methods, concepts and so on?
2. Does your group share a vision of the future, or might there be conflicting views about what you're trying to achieve?
3. Are all the participants making regular, meaningful contributions, in ways that don't cause stress or strain due to their individual needs or interests?
4. Does your group agree on and have clarity concerning the next most-important actions to be taken, and the roles and responsibilities required?
5. Are there participants who, without meaning to, tend to dominate conversations and interactions, and are there participants who don't involve or assert themselves as much as they could or should?
6. Does your group trust that the benefits, rewards and recognition that stem from your collective effort will be or are being fairly distributed?

Finally, if you really want to do everything you can to help your group take positive steps to improve its capability, as you discuss the above questions with them, ask, 'How might we improve?' Use the feedback grid shown in Figure 7, writing your suggestions in the appropriate quadrant.

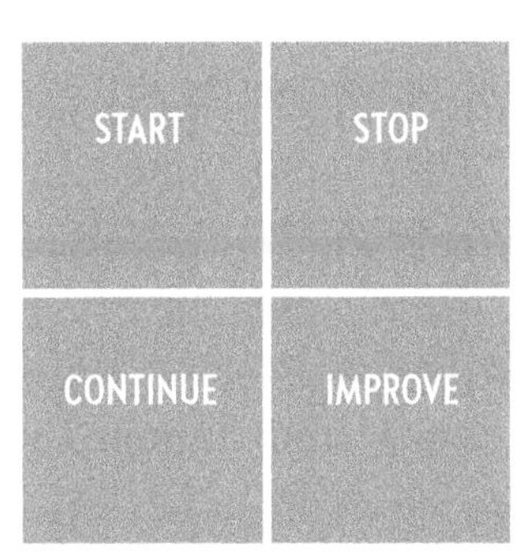

Figure 7. Start–Stop–Continue–Improve Action Grid

As you do this, discuss with the group whether everyone agrees with a given suggestion, and what it would mean to take the necessary action: When could it be done? Does a specific person need to lead or coordinate the effort? How will you know when it has been done well?

This last step can be especially useful if you find that your group has a 'stick in the mud' – someone who, for whatever reason, is limiting the group's ability to move forward. Stepping through the above collaboration challenge questions, then applying the Start–Stop–Continue–Improve action grid, can help people to identify and express their frustrations while exploring actions to resolve them. This in turn will help the rest of the group to generate alignment and begin working more productively – to get them out of the mud, so to speak.

Tool 27: The Perspective Modeller

As I've explained, an understanding of the perspectives of others is central to great collaboration design. In fact, this is what all of the tools in this chapter are about: helping your group surface and engage its collective perspective. But what if, to fulfil the goal of your collaboration, you need to understand the perspective of someone who isn't 'in the room'?

This tool, a common and simple technique that is used by product designers, assists you with this. Often called *empathy modelling*, this process helps you develop a model of another person's attitudes, interests and orientations by considering the different elements that make up that person's perspective.

Use this tool when the success of your collaborative initiative, either in part or in whole, relies on engaging – or delivering value to – an individual or a team not immediately available to your group. I believe that you should learn directly from the source whenever possible, but there are many reasons why it might be difficult (if not impossible) to interact with end users or key stakeholders – in fact, this is more common than you might think.

Also consider using this tool to prepare for engaging with these folks. It provides you with a hypothesis to test, pushing your understanding further than it would otherwise get with these important people.

STEP 1: DO SOME SILENT WRITING

Create a four-quadrant space on a whiteboard, flip chart or projected slide and label each one 'Think', 'Feel', 'Hear' or 'Say' (see Figure 8). Now create a subject (persona), naming and briefly describing them.

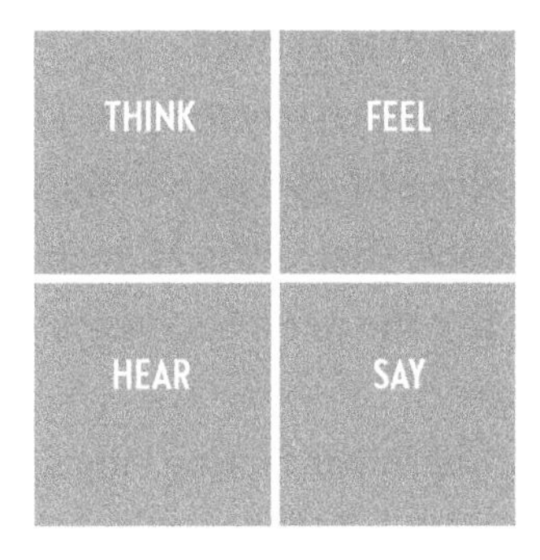

Figure 8. The Perspective Model

Prior to commencing this activity, develop a focus question for participants to answer that roughly follows this formula: 'Regarding X topic, what might [persona name] be thinking, feeling, hearing or saying?' I usually also describe a specific situation to really get the participants thinking, such as: 'They are sharing an elevator ride with a colleague when the subject of the collaboration comes up? What do they hear? How does this make them feel? What do they think? What do they say?'

Then, in the usual fashion, get the group members to jot down one idea per sticky note, giving them about five minutes for this. Encourage them to create one sticky note per quadrant.

STEP 2: CREATE A SHARED VIEW

After your five-minute timer goes off, ask for someone to share a sticky note, passing it up to you as they read it out. Once you've posted it in the relevant quadrant, ask if anyone else has a similar note. Work your way around the group, adding to and discussing one quadrant at a time. For larger groups, make sure you keep up a reasonable pace, with each participant simply reading out their thought. You can time-box a discussion at the end of each quadrant, asking the participants to focus on filling in gaps if some quadrants are less filled in than others.

STEP 3: DISCUSS THE IMPLICATIONS

As you're posting the sticky notes, try to create clusters to highlight any similarities and differences in the views being presented. Encourage a general discussion about what you're all seeing and work towards a synthesised view of what the model is suggesting. Capture the discussion points as you go.

Make sure you highlight conflicting views, if there are any. Have brief discussions about why different assumptions are being made about the perspectives of those you're modelling, and ideally resolve the conflicting view into a single assumption. If you're unable to do this, or if your group is particularly unclear about the perspective the persona holds, discuss ways in which you might gather some validating data. For instance, does one of your participants know someone who is representative of your model, someone they could call or meet with to get their thoughts? Try to think of the simplest, fastest way in which you can learn about that person or get input from them.

Finally, consider the implications for your initiative and your next wave of activity. Are there any aspects of your collaboration or planned activities that need adjustment or reconceptualisation? Don't shy away from having your initiative challenged by the results of your model. It's far better to work through challenges early on than to have key stakeholders angrily revolt against your ideas in a workshop. I've seen this happen, and afterwards, the project rarely recovers. On the other hand, I've also seen collaborative empathy modelling positively transform the appreciation and priorities of a roomful of executives.

A Note on Diversity

Tool 27: The Perspective Modeller is designed to help you understand perspectives that are different from your own. Collaboration, almost by definition, is the alignment and integration of different perspectives into a new shared perspective. But this becomes more difficult as the diversity of perspectives increases. As this happens, it can be tempting to limit participant diversity.

Doing this can be prudent, depending on your situation, but keep in mind that there's the distinct risk of groupthink – the lack of any challenge to the dominant view. This arises almost entirely because of a lack of diversity. It's an anti-collaborative dynamic because, through a homogenous set of views, it limits the opportunities for tension to be raised, and as a result, it limits the potential for the cocreation of shared value through the resolution of that tension.

A true diversity of perspectives, on the other hand, brings more potential to collaboration because it increases the amount and types of tension that might be resolved into shared value. The challenges involved shouldn't be underestimated, of course, but a diversity of perspectives should be considered the primary means of generating productive tension and thus collaborative potential.

So look for opportunities to diversify the make-up of your collaboration, such as along the lines of age, gender, and cultural, ethnic and sociopolitical outlook. Bringing in an *outside* perspective can also do wonders for disrupting counterproductive assumptions your group may be holding about how others will view and value what they're trying to do. Diversity of outlook – outlook being how someone sees the world based on how they've experienced it – is an extremely powerful driver of productive tension, and in turn the value and impact a collaboration can deliver. The trick is to maintain momentum while resolving these productive tensions, which is the focus of the next chapter.

CHAPTER 11

Maintain

There are many reasons why a collaborative group may not stay together long enough to deliver on their value proposition. Attending to a diversity of perspectives and resolving other tensions are among these challenges. But far and away the biggest reason in my experience is simply not making enough compelling progress, fast enough. The four tools in this chapter are designed to help a group of people stay together by keeping the evolving vision focused while generating shared value. If these two things happen, then this is usually enough to keep a group together.

Unlike the tools in Chapter 10, which should be used selectively, I'd recommend always using the tools in this chapter. They are relevant to all collaborations; however, you might scale them up or down depending on your needs and situation.

The first tool in this chapter helps ensure that all of your participants remain on the same page, and that they each have the ability to contribute in a way that doesn't create more work for other individuals. Tool 29: Refocusing and Realising Outcomes then spells out a process for updating your VOA strategy from Tool 19: The Collaboration Plan – you should expect your vision and overall plan to need updating from time to time to keep your group aligned and focused.

Tool 30: The 3Cs Engagement Plan has a similar intent, providing a process for updating your stakeholder map, but with a focus on re-energising your broader stakeholder engagement, as well as refreshing your cocreating core's regular rhythm of activity. The final tool in this chapter prompts you to think carefully about how your larger group is or isn't being inspired and guided by the activity of key individuals in your core. This dynamic can be a virtuous or vicious cycle that can make or break collaborations, especially the larger and longer-term initiatives.

Tool 28: A Single Source of Truth

The purpose of this tool is to create a common accessible reference point, or space, for your initiative's shared plans and outcomes. Think of this as a shared workspace where your participants can cocreate the most important representations of the collaboration, enabling them to sing from the same song sheet, as it were. Having what I call *a single source of truth* is one of the simplest ways of both confirming and generating alignment between participants.

This tool builds on the first principle of collaboration – shared ideas – with an external, common version of what is otherwise held in the minds of the participants, or more often in their individual notebooks and laptops. It also expands on what was started in step 3 of Tool 6: A Draft Collaboration Design, where you developed a first draft of what your collaboration's shared plans and outcomes might look like. Assuming you now have a group to work with, this tool will go beyond the theoretical to create something tangible.

In less-formal settings, a shared communication channel can sometimes suffice as a single source of truth, providing a means of coordination when the group is not together. For more formal but smaller collaborations, certain content outputs are often the focus for a single source of truth, such as communications, a runsheet for a workshop, or slides for a presentation. For larger, more complex collaborations to maintain alignment, a single source of truth will need to cater to all of these, as well as more detailed aspects of planning and execution, such as tracking the progress of tasks and other elements of project management.

STEP 1: START SLOW AND SIMPLE

It's easy to come on too strong when you grasp the importance of having a single source of truth. Certainly, when it works well, it will reduce confusion and any doubling up of effort, while driving alignment and efficiency across the whole group. But the challenge with 'implementing' a single source of truth is that, whatever the solution, it must be wilfully adopted by your participants. The barriers to adoption shouldn't be underestimated either. Therefore, it's a good idea to use collaboration as a strategy for generating the buy-in needed for adoption, as opposed to implementing a tool or approach and expecting everyone to simply jump on board.

Start by answering the following questions with your group:

1. What are the critical pieces of content we're working on that we should all have access to? (This could be a planning document, presentation slides, an event plan, creative work ... really, anything that's the subject of cocreation.)
2. What methods and tools for sharing and cocreation do we already have experience with, and will they support the sharing and cocreation of our critical content? Are there better solutions, not necessarily technological ones?
3. How will the access to, and integration of, contributions work? Will one person need to manage this, or can the responsibility be distributed? (The latter is preferable.)

Gently temper any enthusiastic calls for large systems by asking, 'What's the simplest first step we can take to try that?' One approach we typically use at Collabforge when beginning a new collaborative project is to create a *source code deck* – a slide deck where we capture and then share everything that's meaningful. The format of presentation slides lends itself well to engagement and consumption, as the slides aren't as dense as a document. If someone has missed a meeting, they can quickly get an update by logging on and looking at the source code deck. We then progress to more-complex formats when the slide deck clearly starts to fail to hold the content appropriately.

STEP 2: LEAD BY EXAMPLE

Even after your participants have decided how they'll share and cocreate via a single source of truth, it can be difficult for them to change their behaviours in order to adopt new processes and tools. At the outset, assume that you'll have to do more than your fair share of the work to keep things organised and on track, process-wise, and to demonstrate the key behaviours.

A simple technique is to start and end working sessions by returning to your single source of truth as a group, to make sure that anything of value you've generated – decisions, ideas, insights, content and so on – is captured there. If more processing is required to capture your work outputs – for example, transcribing a wall covered in sticky notes – then call it out as a piece of work in order to get it resourced. Don't let the group get comfortable with you doing the integration work. If this happens, you'll eventually feel either overloaded or resentful, or both, which may jeopardise your initiative.

Having said this, give your group plenty of latitude and support in the early stages of adoption. And constantly ask yourself: 'Am I demonstrating the ideal behaviours that others need to follow, in order for our single source of truth to be maintained and to function well?'

STEP 3: BUILD OUT AND STAY DISCIPLINED

Once your group has gained a little experience in building and maintaining a single source of truth, you can begin to progressively extend it by adding a file structure, types of formats, even different platforms and complementary tools. But don't go overboard – it's easier to keep a small house clean than a large one! Simplicity will help your group stay focused on what matters: creating quality content, integrating inputs and keeping things generally organised.

For larger or longer projects with more participants and content, you may need to schedule the occasional working bee to reorganise or update the content in your single source of truth. The efficiency and alignment that comes from all participants being able to quickly find what they need, and importantly to find the same thing, shouldn't be misjudged. It's like the role that oil plays in an engine. Its job is to keep things turning over smoothly. Without it, the engine will grind to a halt.

A Note on Technology Adoption

The adoption of technology, whether for a single source of truth or anything else, can be fraught, with great potential for a breakdown. I liken it to using a hammer for the first time to get serious work done, like building a shed. If you've never used one, then despite its simplicity, you're bound to end up with some bent nails and probably a bruised thumb. I've been in a great many professional situations where everyone was absolutely sure that a given technology would 'just work' and be loved by all, only to find out that the opposite was true.

Keep in mind that the adoption of collaboration technology is a social phenomenon. It involves feedback loops of users considering the adoption preferences of other users in considering their own decision to adopt. This process is not logical, rational or assured. Further, the frustration that one person encounters can spread through a group via the technology itself, undermining goodwill and generating even more negative adoption dynamics.

However, when technology serves a high-value purpose, or solves a clear and present problem, then even if there are hiccups in adoption, people are much more likely to maintain their patience while these are worked through. They'll also be much more likely to place the blame for these hiccups on bad interfaces or user error, as opposed to you or the collaboration design.

So go slow and do plenty of testing to make sure you're very familiar with the tech and the approach. Also consider getting your most enthusiastic and/or influential participants on board before everyone else. These folks will help others overcome the obstacles that are almost certain to pop up, either by stepping up with tech support or by inspiring them to make the required effort.

Tool 29: Refocusing and Realising Outcomes

The realisation of high-value outcomes gives a huge boost to collaborative activity and group cohesion. I know this is obvious, but it's surprising how often outcomes get lost in the mix. This tool will keep your group focused on the right outcomes and making steady progress in achieving them.

STEP 1: TEST THE IMPACT OF YOUR OUTCOMES AND OUTPUTS

The first step in assessing whether your group is focused on the highest-value outcomes is to spend a moment contemplating just what you consider an outcome to be. I find it useful to separate the real-world creations your group will produce from the intangible changes in people's minds and experiences – the former I designate as outputs, the latter as outcomes or impacts. This distinction, which I first made in Chapter 4, is useful because real-world outputs are almost always the means to an outcome. We create a piece of software to enable new interactions. We create a work of art to engage and move our audience. We create a new strategy to align activity for competitive advantage. We create a new policy to generate better societal conditions.

Revisit your VOA strategy from Tool 19: The Collaboration Plan and review each outcome to make sure that it's in line with the above definition. If you discover an output, simply extrapolate up to the intended outcome that it's meant to generate. Feel free to keep your outputs listed in your VOA, as they're important for triangulating your outcomes and activities. However, move them down, below outcomes and above activities. Typically, an activity will produce an output, which will generate an outcome.

Having established that the outcomes conform to the specific definition, you can begin prioritising them. But first be aware, as introduced in Tool 6: A Draft Collaboration Design, that collaborative outcomes are often multidimensional, with participants seeing different points of value in the same outcome. This means that what's written down can't always be taken at face value. Discuss with your group what they value about a given outcome, what it means to them, and why realising it matters. The goal here is to confirm that everyone is on the same page regarding what an outcome is and why it's important.

With your outcomes now well understood, prioritise them to focus on the most important ones. Write each outcome on a separate sticky note, then draw the matrix in Figure 9 on a whiteboard. Place your notes in the appropriate quadrants, discussing them as a group and noting the ratings. Those that rank 1 or 2 deserve the most focus in order to realise your activities.

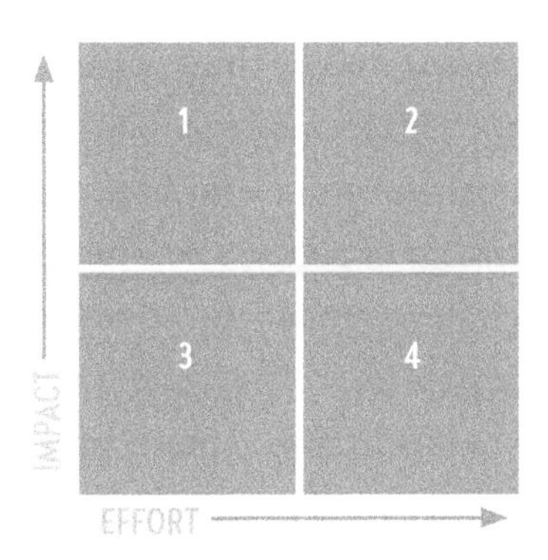

Figure 9. Outcome Prioritisation Matrix

You should now feel confident about your highest-value outcomes. If you don't, keep at it until you do. Agreeing on which outcomes are the most important is essentially the same thing as agreeing on why you're collaborating. This agreement is one of the most valuable things that a collaboration design provides.

STEP 2: PROTOTYPE ITERATIVELY

Now turn your attention to accelerating the realisation of these outcomes. Because collaboration is time- and energy-intensive, it's imperative to always be looking for ways in which to fast-track your outcomes. This doesn't mean rushing them to completion, but you should certainly keep up the pressure to bring them about, otherwise participants will feel that things are dragging on and they may drift away before you reach your goal.

Prototyping is one of the best ways of bringing the future forward and realising an early version of your outcomes. Even a prototype output will generate an outcome. And if you've done a good job in step 1 of this tool, your participants will value this outcome, even if it's a smaller version of your ultimate vision. Importantly, prototyped outcomes can give you enough of a feeling of achievement to confirm that you're pointed in the right direction. You can and should use this information to course-correct and make improvements to your plan and vision.

Because a prototype isn't the real thing, it can take a range of forms, all of which may differ from the final version. This allows you to zero in on, and model, critical aspects of your final outcome; for example, certain sections of a strategy or policy; a non-functional graphic design of a software interface; or a smaller, scaled-back version of an event with trusted audience members. Deciding what to prototype with your group can be just as fruitful as actually prototyping it, as it will reveal the value propositions and priorities of all involved.

This step involves taking the outcomes from step 1 that were ranked 1 or 2 and challenging all participants to refer to them in developing four different prototype ideas. Get everyone to divide a sheet of paper into four by folding it, set a timer for four minutes, and have the participants jot down four ideas: one in each quadrant of their piece of paper. A simple title for each idea will suffice, but encourage participants to also do basic sketches to bring the ideas to life. When the timer goes off, get each person to quickly share their ideas, at the same time encouraging others to call out if they have duplicate or related ideas.

After everyone has had a turn, using either the impact–effort matrix from step 1 or by simply deciding as a group, identify one or two ideas that will be highly beneficial to prototype, within the constraints of the available time and resources. The participants should be confident that whatever is chosen for prototyping will provide valuable insights regarding your final vision, and this should be quickly and easily achievable. Remember, in this activity you're trying to remove as much friction as possible in pulling your future outcomes into the present.

STEP 3: ADJUST YOUR ACTIVITY FOR PRODUCTIVITY

Now that you've refocused your outcomes and have one or more clear prototyping opportunities, review your group's activity and productivity. For collaborative initiatives, it's worth periodically assessing your productivity, as less-traditional management is often involved in making improvements. Group work routines and approaches need refinement at different stages and for different goals and conditions, especially as your collaborative capability improves. Having some prototypes to deliver can supply a boost of inspiration to make sure your group is working well.

To evaluate your group's productivity, answer and discuss the following questions:

1. How often does the cocreating core get together and do real work? Is this enough?

2 Are any key participants regularly missing from these sessions? How might they be better included?
3 Is there a different meeting time or frequency that would better suit your core group's current needs?
4 Is your working environment inspiring, or at least conducive to inspiration? How could it be improved?
5 When your core is together, what's the balance of talking versus working? Is the group productive? How can you all be more productive when you're together?
6 Can you identify any barriers that are blocking the realisation of your prototypes or outcomes, or negatively impacting your productivity?

As your group discusses these questions, ask the participants to jot down the ideas they feel strongly about on sticky notes and organise them against the Start–Stop–Continue–Improve matrix (see Figure 10) that was introduced in step 3 of Tool 26: A Collaboration Self-Assessment. This will help your participants agree on what changes might be made to improve your working practices. Change is never easy, so consider as a group the value of a particular improvement – specifically, how it will help you more quickly and effectively realise your prototypes or outcomes.

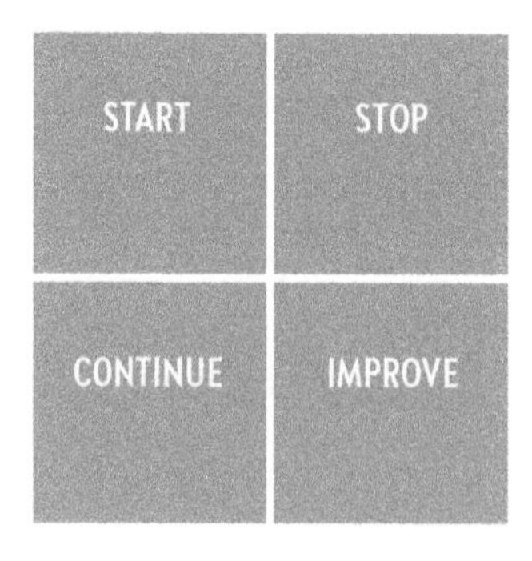

Figure 10. Start–Stop–Continue–Improve Action Grid

Once you've decided on what changes to make, consider how this would be best done. When you have accepted habits and routines in place, change will always meet resistance. You may need to remind the participants down the track of your collective agreement to a particular change, or assign someone the task of calling everyone to account when you arrive at the moment when a change must occur. You might insert a standing agenda point for when your group gets together, to check in on how these changes are progressing. Ultimately, though, what really matters here is that your group members are learning together and changing for the better as a result.

Tool 30: The 3Cs Engagement Plan

The interactions within and across your 3Cs stakeholder groups – the cocreating core, the cooperating community and the coordinated crowd – will dictate how your collaboration generates its value and impact. That means, just like the need to occasionally revise your VOA strategy, at times you'll have to revisit your engagement map, originally created using Tool 8: Participant Mapping for the Core, Community and Crowd, then developed collaboratively using Tool 20: Detailed Participation Map and Core Formation.

This tool provides a process for this while developing a compelling, realistic and regular means of engaging the people in these three groups. This engagement is one of the best ways of maintaining momentum in your collaboration, as well as keeping your thinking fresh and your group focused.

STEP 1: UPDATE YOUR 3CS STAKEHOLDER MAP

Revisit the map you generated through Tool 20: the list of potential participants organised under three headings equivalent to the 3Cs stakeholders. Now rework and build out the people and organisations listed in the three categories, adding new participants and removing those you now know shouldn't be there. You can do this collaboratively in a group setting, or you can have the first crack at it yourself and get your fellow collaborators to review your work afterwards.

As a refresher, the core is the engine of your collaboration, driving the hard day-to-day work and the cocreation of key ideas, decisions and outcomes. The cooperating community operates in a much more-transactional fashion, taking as inputs what the core generates in order to create value-adding outputs to pass back into the core. Finally, the coordinated crowd doesn't need to specifically *do* anything, other than (ideally) being receptive to your communications, whatever the message may be.

STEP 2: ENGAGE THE COMMUNITY AND THE CROWD

Now that you've refreshed your stakeholder map, consider how each of the three groups might be better engaged. As your initiative matures, so too will the opportunities for involvement – this is just as true for the core as it is for the crowd. But keep in mind that it will be easy to overlook those furthest from the core. It can be particularly tempting to put off engagement with the crowd. You may feel that you're not quite ready to do this, but you'll probably never feel 100 per cent ready. While this sentiment is natural, it's really not productive to give in to it.

The most effective collaborations engage all three groups from the beginning, and they do it consistently, strategically and iteratively, building out their reach and depth of engagement as they go. This is the goal you should strive for: growing your engagement progressively with all three groups from the outset, not sequentially.

As you consider engaging the community and crowd, remember to focus on *their* interests as much as yours. You'll naturally gravitate towards your value proposition over theirs, so if you don't consciously and explicitly consider their interests, you could overlook them. If this happens, at best you risk missing the opportunity to get more of what you want out of them; at worst, you risk putting them off your initiative, or not getting their attention at all.

To overcome this bias, apply Tool 9: The Double-Sided Value Proposition when considering engagement activities. As a group, brainstorm answers to the following questions:

1. How might we, for our core, provide better experiences in cocreation, connection and productivity?
2. How might we, for our community, provide value-adding, transactional-type interactions for those who can most contribute to, appreciate or benefit from our initiative?
3. How might we, for our crowd, provide easy and enjoyable opportunities for as many like-minded people as possible to learn about what we're doing and why?

Now use your answers to fill in Table 3.

1 Cocreating core	[Individual or group name]	[Activity]	[Our value proposition]	[Their value proposition]
2 Cooperating community	[Individual or group name]	[Activity]	[Our value proposition]	[Their value proposition]
3 Coordinated crowd	[Individual or group name]	[Activity]	[Our value proposition]	[Their value proposition]

Table 3. A 3Cs Engagement Plan Template

Your table should end up looking like Table 4:

1 Cocreating core	Jane	Hold every other weekly working session near her office	Get more of her time	She's able to more easily make the commute
2 Cooperating community	Central IT group	Lunchtime feedback session	Keep them involved and flag risks early	Their input is recognised and valued (and there's a yummy lunch)
3 Coordinated crowd	Interested individuals browsing our website	Newsletter	A means of discovering who they are and staying connected	Learn more about our subject matter and initiative

Table 4. Example of a 3Cs Engagement Plan

Don't limit yourself to answering only the above questions. Feel free to brainstorm any that you feel are more relevant to your situation. You know your setting, people and opportunities best, so draw on this.

Your participants should ask, 'What's blocking us from more fully engaging with any or all of the three groups?' Make a list of the things that can be done to unblock yourselves, and put dates and leaders against these tasks. Engagement is often the actual work of progressing a collaborative initiative, so if you're getting too caught up in not being able to interact beyond your core, you likely risk stagnation.

STEP 3: MAINTAIN A REGULAR RHYTHM OF ENGAGEMENT

The last step is to refine and confirm the viability and impact of your engagement plan. The hardest part of planning is execution – most plans never get fully implemented – so you want to make sure you get the most value out of the plan, and that you can actually do it in the first place. You need to rank your engagement ideas regarding the effort involved and the impact, then sequence them, to decide if the plan is viable and contributes to a regular rhythm of activity.

To begin with, consider each activity against the matrix in Figure 11. Ask yourself if an activity will have a big impact on your initiative's success. Will it require considerable effort and resources? Now give your activities a ranking of 1 to 4.

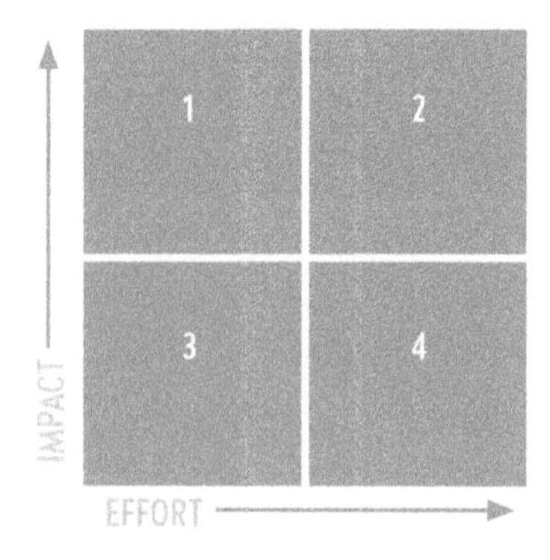

Figure 11. Engagement Impact/Effort Prioritisation Matrix

Before making any decisions regarding your activities, take a second pass, this time considering them from the perspective of the individuals or groups involved. Do they have the ability to influence your attempts at success? Down the track, might they make something important happen, or get others involved, by participating? Does your initiative align with their goals or interests? Give your activities a ranking of A to D (see Figure 12).

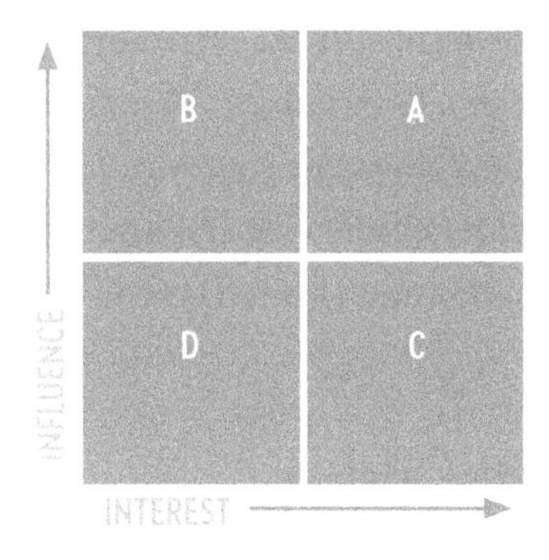

Figure 12. Engagement Influence/Interest Prioritisation Matrix

Now consider the activities with the highest combined score (1A) and discuss these as a group. Regarding the activities with lower scores, can you imagine ways of improving their impact, reducing the effort they require, or involving participants with higher levels of influence and interest? Refine your activities until you feel you have a compelling collection, with several activities in each of your core, community and crowd lists.

Finally, sequence your activities in a timeline, duplicating those that repeat; for example, a monthly newsletter. Ideally, do this on a whiteboard or a tabletop using sticky notes. If you developed a timeline of activities as part of step 3 in Tool 19: The Collaboration Plan, consider using that as a starting point, or updating it with the results of the current step. In either case, it's important to see all of the activities together, in order, to find out if there are overlaps that will cause resourcing issues or clash with important dates or holidays. You also need to make sure that there aren't any big gaps in the timeline, where months go by without any engagement beyond the core – unless there's a very good reason for this.

Once you have your timeline of validated activities, translate it into your single source of truth. First, though, consider the best format for this: if your plan isn't too complex, a few graphical elements in a presentation slide may suffice; at the other end of the spectrum, you can use a spreadsheet or a Gantt chart. Whatever you choose, make sure it's integrated with your single source of truth. Your core participants' access to, and interaction with, a shared plan is central to their sense of shared ownership, and ultimately their sense of responsibility for its delivery.

Tool 31: An Activity Catalyst

Even with a strong plan for engagement, keeping participants genuinely and actively engaged can be difficult, whether they're in your cocreating core, cooperating community or coordinated crowd. It gets even harder if your collaboration requires significant scaling using online tools. The need to create a large collaborative community, online or otherwise, is one of the more compelling reasons to collaborate in the first place, but getting to the point where good numbers of people are regularly contributing is a big challenge.

In every collaborative situation, the primary driver of group activity is ... group activity, which is a nice little chicken-or-the-egg situation. This is often resolved by an individual whose actions serve to inspire and motivate others to contribute – an *activity catalyst.* A single person's enthusiastic participation can be highly infectious. This role is especially important in the early stages of collaboration, but it never really ceases to matter.

You should think of this role as a function of collaborative leadership. Therefore, in order to maintain the momentum of your initiative, you need to make sure this role is assigned and resourced. In many cases, this will prove to be a natural role for one or more of the people at the centre of the collaboration, those who tend to contribute more, and better, than everyone else. In other cases, this role can even be hired in professionally. This tool will help you assess the requirements of this role and its resourcing.

STEP 1: ASSESS THE NEED FOR AN ACTIVITY CATALYST

Not all collaborations require an explicitly nominated activity catalyst. But all collaborations rely on this dynamic. Someone has to contribute first to get things moving, and someone has to contribute *well* for others to know what this looks like. And once your initiative is underway, it will naturally go through more- and-less active periods, with the latter requiring someone to kick things back into gear.

If you have a very active group, then you may not even notice that this is taking place; in fact, you may only need to pick up the slack here and there, when needed. If you're in the early stages of establishing a group, at least recognise the significance of this role and support whomever in your group is playing it. You might consider taking up this role yourself, to make absolutely sure it's covered.

If, however, your group or its extended stakeholder cohort is particularly shy, busy, large or otherwise disengaged, I recommend you discuss with your core group how to best resource an explicit activity catalyst role. This person should make regular, visible, high-quality contributions, as well as encouraging and supporting others to do the same. You should also consider the life cycle of your collaboration and any requirements you might have to drive activity at later stages.

To determine your activity catalyst needs, answer and discuss the following questions with your core.

1. What does 'active contribution' mean regarding our core, as well as our community and crowd?
2. When will we most need it, and what will be at risk if we don't get it?
3. Are there natural activity catalysts in our core or the larger group who can play this role well? How can we support them to do so?

STEP 2: CREATE A PLAN

Develop a plan grounded in your answers to the above questions that accounts for, at a minimum, who will do what and when. It could be as simple as, 'Jane is going to take the lead on making the first contributions to our strategy document, and then she'll email and call those in our core who haven't made contributions within two weeks'. On the other hand, you might be trying to kick-start an online community. So you'll assign this role to several people who take it in turns to make regular posts to your social media channels, with yet another person taking on dedicated engagement with your VIP contributors.

Make sure the focus is on keeping the ideas and information flowing, as well as curating and promoting quality contributions from others. This might well be a 'Fake it till you make it' type of strategy, where an effort is made to drive activity until it is able to continue under its own steam. Alternatively, you can take more of a maintenance approach, with triggers or thresholds for low levels of activity that spark your activity catalysts into action. Regardless, do your best to keep the plan as simple as possible. It needs to be realistic, even conservative, if your catalysts are to maintain enthusiastic levels of activity.

STEP 3: REFLECT AND REVIEW PERIODICALLY

Because the purpose of an activity catalyst is to create a positive feedback loop that inspires and stimulates activity, you need to periodically review and reflect on what's working and what isn't. You won't get this right straight out of the gate. Different groups need different prompts at different stages of their collaboration.

To review and refine the impact of the activity catalyst, ask the following questions:

1. What are some recent examples of activity being catalysed?
2. When and why did this happen?
3. What can be learned from this and how might it be replicated?
4. Can a simple test be created to see if these successful dynamics can be replicated?

An experiment driven by a simple hypothesis is a very effective means of learning what best drives activity in your group. For example, your hypothesis might be this: 'If I post a message to our online group specifically asking for an individual's contribution on X topic, they will respond, which stimulates others to contribute'. Now see if your hypothesis can be validated, or if it needs to be changed.

Beware of distributing the role of activity catalyst among the group members on the assumption that everyone can effectively 'chip in' where and when needed, without coordination. This rarely works, except perhaps in very small collaborations. What's more likely to happen is that this role and the attached responsibilities will end up falling on someone's shoulders without the proper support or recognition. Worse still, no-one will attend to it and your collaboration will suffer. Keep in mind your response to the question, 'What are we risking if we don't get the activity we're planning for?'

Catalysing effective participation is such an important dynamic for collaboration that, along with the facilitation of a single source of truth, it's one of the core services that Collabforge provides for clients – even when they haven't asked for it and are unaware we're doing it. We're always conscious of modelling great participation and ensuring that it gets resourced in line with the needs of the project.

I recall one project with a state government client where catalysing participation was the primary goal. We developed a collaboration design for the creation of a large social media–driven community focused on emergency services volunteer information and support. In order to get quality community participation, we hired 25 aligned and interested university students to help with the job, training them in what great participation looks like, then set them loose, with our own team acting as their activity catalyst. Within four weeks we had attracted about 10,000 participants who were catalysed and contributing across three different social media channels. Eight years on, that community is still going strong, now with some 20,000 participants.

While having an effective strategy for catalysing participation was essential in achieving this growth, it was not the only element required. The following chapter explores more of the considerations involved in growing your collaboration.

CHAPTER 12

Grow

Catalysing participation is most important for collaboration designs that aim to grow their membership above 25 participants, into a category that I call *mass collaboration*. Books like *Wikinomics* (2006) by Anthony D Williams and *Here Comes Everybody* (2008) by Clay Shirky make much of the opportunity to 'harness the crowd' for productive collaborative outcomes at scale. In fact, initiatives such as Wikipedia suggest the remarkable potential of massive-scale collaborative participation due to the small contributions of a great many people (although many Wikipedians have contributed significantly to the initiative, no doubt acting as activity catalysts). Such initiatives reach a tipping point, and the social proof of participation becomes a powerful positive feedback loop that drives many thousands of people to participate.

In this chapter, regarding the final stage of the Collabforge method, we'll take a pragmatic approach to growing your collaboration, whether this means adding another dozen participants, or adding another thousand. Having been involved in a number of projects that have set their sights on mass collaboration, I can tell you that it's very challenging to make this happen. If this is your aim, I'd urge you to temper your enthusiasm with the obvious point that growing a collaboration to such a large size takes far more work, time and energy than it does to get one off the ground with half-a-dozen people.

With that caveat out of the way, it is exactly the point of this book to help make more mass collaborations possible. Incredible things are possible when many people are aligned and inspired to cocreate together. But you need an eyes-wide-open conscious awareness of what you're trying to do, and a foundation of shared capability inside a high-performing cocreating core.

The first tool in this chapter provides a way of understanding how collaboration can grow when scaling up membership. At the same time, it will help you assess where you are now in this process, and what it might look like to grow. Tool 33: A Growth Assessment will then assist you in making a sensible decision about incorporating strategic growth into your collaboration design.

Tool 34: Onboarding Participants gives you the means to address the greatest challenge of growth: bringing new participants into the fold efficiently and effectively. This is the primary barrier and bottleneck to large-scale collaboration. The next tool will help you consider the most appropriate technologies for meeting your scaling needs and goals. The final tool presented in this book focuses on when to stop collaborating. Most collaborations will eventually run their course, but this isn't always an easy assessment to make.

Tool 32: The Golden Staircase

This tool will teach you about how growth works in collaboration, as well as what growth might look like for your initiative. Most collaborations benefit from some amount of growth, so if this tool sparks ideas, or if growth is a clear objective for you, then Tool 33: A Growth Assessment will help you consolidate your plans.

A number of years ago at Collabforge, we developed the framework we now call The Golden Staircase. I can't exactly remember why we gave it this funny name, probably because of the promise that scalable collaboration holds for our projects, for business, even for humanity. Regardless, the name stuck, and we've now used this framework to understand, design and support hundreds of collaborations. The thing that has stood out in this time is that, while successfully stepping up the staircase indeed represents the 'gold' to be had, this is not without significant challenges. This tool and the following two tools will help you break down and deal with these.

STEP 1: ASSESS YOUR POSITION ON THE STAIRCASE

Growth is a function of the third principle of collaboration: shared capability. Collaboration can only grow in conjunction with the capability that a group has to communicate their vision and intent, demonstrate social proof for participation, onboard new participants, and integrate their new contributions. If some or all of these capabilities are weak, then the growth will be weak too. On the flipside, the more capability a group has, the faster that group can scale.

More generally, bringing on new members will always be difficult because this necessarily introduces tension. There's the tension of new questions, ideas and perspectives to understand. There's the tension of having someone new contest your assumptions, ideas and approaches. And there's the tension of having to stop being productive so you can explain your initiative to someone and introduce them to how things are done. This means that, even as the capability to grow builds in a group of people, they will only be able to handle so much of this tension at any one time before they cease to be productive altogether.

For these reasons, collaboration scales incrementally, organically even. Figure 13 gives you a sense of what this looks like. The rising numbers in the increasingly bigger circles – you might recognise this as the Fibonacci sequence, where each number is the sum of the previous two numbers – are indicative of the incremental growth pattern that we've experienced many times at Collabforge. Once you've successfully added a few people to your group, you'll be able to add a few more the next time, because your capability to grow will have increased through this process.

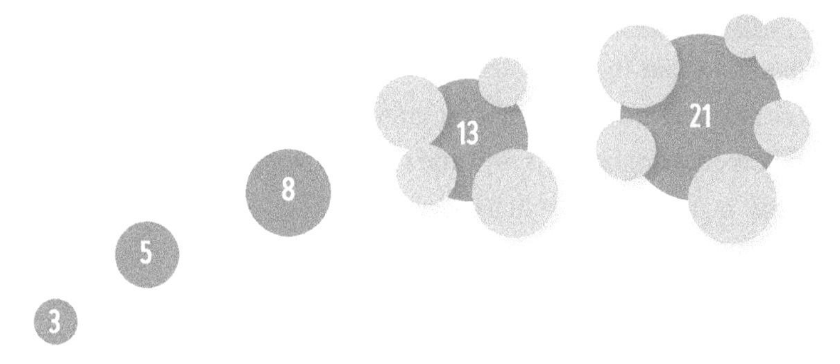

Figure 13. The Golden Staircase of Collaborative Growth

The sub-circles that have been added to the circles numbered '13' and '21' indicate another aspect of growth you need to be aware of; that is, the notion that, as groups get larger, sub-groups naturally form. This has been written about in the context of social network theory and is called Reed's Law. To paraphrase, Reed's Law states that, as a social network gets larger, so does the potential for sub-groups, and as sub-groups form, the value of this network gets exponentially greater. In other words, sub-groups are to be expected and welcomed because they're like parallel processors, adding exponentially more value to your collaboration.

I like to call Reed's Law the 'dinner party dynamic'. If you've ever had to get the attention of a dinner party of a dozen people or so, you'll know that it's not easy to do. This is because you can have six or so separate conversations happening in parallel, and making quite a racket! This points to the challenge that sub-groups pose to collaboration – for every sub-group that forms, new and different tensions potentially can be introduced. There's then a greater potential for these sub-groups to resolve their tensions in ways that can go in different directions to what you were hoping for, such as away from other sub-groups, pulling your collaboration apart. On the other hand, more sub-group tension means more potential for shared value to be generated through the resolution of these tensions, which is exactly what Reed's Law points to.

This tool is designed to help you make a calculated, strategic decision about growth, given the issues it poses. To begin with, I'd like you to consider where you feel you might be in your growth trajectory. For example, you may be at a point prior to the '3' circle, with an idea that you have yet to communicate to anyone. Or you may be one step beyond this, already working in a small team.

For example, there's a new music project that I'm working on, and myself and another person have just successfully onboarded our third participant. While it has taken a while to figure out if we've been successful, we now believe that we have a foundation of shared capability – vision for the project, songs under our belt, a rehearsal routine and so on – and we're contemplating bringing in two more people. As this example suggests, locating yourself in the growth curve essentially means assessing how many individuals are currently involved and what your plans might be for involving more people.

As discussed in Chapter 6, for the FutureMelbourne city planning project, Collabforge immediately realised that there was a natural progression to scaling from two (the city's manager of strategic planning and myself) to the rest of the world via online engagement. This sequence progressed from us to the steering committee, the planning team, other key internal units, the whole city administration, key external stakeholders, and finally to the local and global public. Mapping out this sequence in advance enabled us to progressively build the capability to onboard each new cohort, learning as we went, and with each step taken putting us on a stronger footing.

STEP 2: DECIDE HOW FAR YOU WANT TO GO

Let's turn our attention to what further growth might look like for you. If you have a live project, what has the process of growth been like so far? Has this been challenging or did it feel easy? Was it planned and strategic, or spontaneous and opportunistic? Take a minute to consider these questions.

Alternatively, if you're considering a collaboration but haven't yet begun it, are you clear on who you would like to bring on board first? If not, do you have ideas about what types of people they might be? In either case, does the notion of bringing in your first participants feel daunting or exciting? Again, take a minute to reflect – turning over these questions will help prime your thinking for the considerations to follow.

Collaborative growth has different implications for the cocreating core, cooperating community and coordinated crowd. Regarding the core, bringing more people into the cocreation process will involve more energy and alignment than having more participants support your efforts in the community through cooperation. It's a similar scenario, if not more dramatic, for the coordinated crowd, where the effort and energy required for social interaction is considerably less. For example, bringing more people into your crowd might involve something as simple as putting a message in someone else's newsletter. Therefore, when considering coordination specifically, The Golden Staircase applies less, in that larger, less-incremental jumps in participation can happen.

Think about what growth might mean for you regarding each of the 3Cs. Do a back-of-an-envelope type of calculation to consider what the maximum memberships might be for your core, community and crowd – obviously, expect the numbers to get progressively bigger as you extend out from your core to your crowd.

For the new music collaboration I mentioned in step 2, I can imagine growing the existing core from three to five (a few more musicians), with the community adding another half-dozen (a sound engineer, producer, publicist, graphic artist, photographer, booking agent), and the crowd extending into the hundreds, possibly thousands (audience members at gigs, listeners online and so on).

Jot down your thoughts, as I've just done, about the number of participants for each of the 3Cs in your collaboration:

1 Core: ______________________________
2 Community: __________________________
3 Crowd: _____________________________

STEP 3: ASSESS THE OPPORTUNITIES FOR TAKING A NEXT STEP

Now consider what a next step might look like for each of the 3Cs. As you think about this, ask yourself if there will be dependencies across the 3Cs that you'll need to be aware of. For example, you may not be ready to extend your community until you've taken a next step by extending your core (as is the case with the music project I mentioned above).

These types of dependencies are to be expected. But that said, always look out for how you might short-circuit them; that is, accelerate the interaction with your community and crowd. An all-too-common blocker in collaborative growth is feeling that you can't interact with your crowd until something important happens with your core or community. Use the prototyping thinking introduced at the start of Chapter 5 and in Tool 29: Refocusing and Realising Outcomes to help break through these barriers.

Taking into consideration the interdependencies and how you might bring forward all of the 3Cs as soon as possible, write down what your next step might be for each (prototypes are welcome!):

1 Core: ______________________________
2 Community: __________________________
3 Crowd: _____________________________

You should now have a basic feel for what growth looks like for you, and what your opportunities are. Let's take these ideas into the next tool to make a conscious and strategic decision regarding growth.

Tool 33: A Growth Assessment

To begin with, let's make an assessment of your collaborative growth needs and requirements. Any decision to try to grow participation should be aligned with your needs, interests and capabilities.

STEP 1: WHAT DO YOU NEED MOST: FUN, POTENTIAL OR SUPPORT?

The idea in step 1 is to better understand what you might get out of involving more people in your collaboration. You can answer the following questions yourself, but ideally, pose them to your group members and get their input. You might consider turning this into a structured group activity as in Tool 13: Individual Perspectives, by replacing the questions in that tool with those presented here.

Fun: Would your experience or that of the others in your group be better if there were more participants to interact with? For example, would you be more energised, or value meeting new people and making more friends in the context of collaboration?

1 Yes
2 Maybe
3 No

If you answered 'Yes' or 'Maybe', who might these new participants be? Make a list. If you don't have specific people in mind, then use generalised profiles to try to understand them.

Potential: Are there skills, experiences or capabilities that are missing, or that could take your group's potential to another level?

1 Yes
2 Maybe
3 No

As for the 'Fun' questions, if you answered 'Yes' or 'Maybe', make a list of who these participants could be. Again, use generalised profiles if you don't have specific people in mind, adding detail regarding their skills and profile; for example, 'Mid-career professionals in the entertainment industry with an interest in giving back to the community', or 'Young government policy wonks, interested in influencing the public debate regarding aged care policy'.

Support: Will some or all of your ambitions require substantive support, sign-off or advocacy from influential people who aren't yet involved?

1 Yes
2 Maybe
3 No

Again, make a list of potential participants. Once you've tackled these questions by yourself or with your group, review your answers to get a feel for what they're saying to you. You can use the following questions to help you understand the implications:

1 Where are the most compelling growth opportunities, from a *needs* basis?
2 Do any of the individuals or groups listed stand out as particularly influential, and are they likely to be interested?
3 What are the no-brainers for growth? Are there also higher-impact but higher-effort opportunities?

STEP 2: WHERE DO YOU NEED GROWTH: IN THE CORE, COMMUNITY OR CROWD?

With the assessment from step 1 in mind, let's turn our attention to where these growth opportunities might have the biggest impact for you – in your core, community or crowd.

The core is where energy-intensive, time-consuming cocreation happens. Review all three sets of questions in step 1, and wherever you answered 'Yes' or 'Maybe', look to the details of these responses and assess if the opportunities you identified rely on or benefit from involvement in your core's cocreation activities. If they do, can you see these people making the commitment to participate in this way?

1 Yes
2 Maybe
3 No

Make a list of those who fall into the 'Yes' and 'Maybe' categories.

Your cooperative community provides for more-transactional exchanges and so lower-intensity engagement demands. However, participants in this category require careful guidance and briefing, which also requires resourcing.

Taking the same approach as above, reviewing where you answered 'Yes' or 'Maybe' in step 1, decide if these potential participants feel like candidates for cooperation. Can you imagine them being willing and able to participate in a more transactional way? (In more-transactional settings, where the sense of shared ownership is less of a factor, you may need to consider if they'll need compensation in some form.) And does cooperation feel like a good fit for some of your opportunities?

1 Yes
2 Maybe
3 No

Make a list of those who fall into the 'Yes' and 'Maybe' categories.

The last category to consider for this step is the coordinated crowd. They aren't on the hook for anything, but they're still a critical force for spreading word-of-mouth awareness for mass collaborations, as well as influencing others to participate through social proof. In addition, the crowd is a staging ground for those who might get involved in the community or core at a later date. All of which is to say that a strong crowd is essential for mass collaborations to reach scale.

Go through your lists from step 1 and make a new list of individuals or groups that fall into coordination-type participation. Regarding those in your crowd, there's an opportunity to dramatically extend your reach by using methods other than one-to-one and face-to-face communication. Coordination lends itself well to campaign-style, en-masse engagement; for example, making use of advertising, social media, email newsletters and the like.

You should now have three lists, each of which includes the participants you brainstormed in step 1 of this tool, but expanded and organised under each of the 3Cs.

STEP 3: UPDATE YOUR ENGAGEMENT PLAN

Let's return to your stakeholder map and activity plan, which you last updated as part of Tool 30: The 3Cs Engagement Plan. Compare the lists you made for opportunities and participants in step 2, organised under each of the 3Cs with your stakeholder map, and review and discuss the following questions with your group:

1. Do you see any risks or opportunities associated with bringing any of these new individuals or groups together with those already involved?
2. How might you address the risks?
3. How might you make more of the opportunity to bring these people together?

Now bring your activity plan into play:

1. How do you think these potential participants would like to be engaged?
2. Do any of your new ideas suggest clashes or cross-impacts with existing or planned activities?

3 Are there new activity ideas that would positively align with, reinforce, or otherwise contribute to your previously planned activities?
4 Would adding the highest-impact ideas have significant resourcing implications? How might you address these?

Use these questions and the group discussion to update your stakeholder map and activity plan. Also consider whether these updates create an opportunity for new outcomes, which can be especially valuable regarding your efforts. Consider all of this carefully as a group, and if you're all in agreement, update your VOA plan accordingly.

Tool 34: Onboarding Participants

As discussed in Tool 32: The Golden Staircase, as well as in many other places in this book, adding new participants to your collaboration is a source of considerable tension. At a minimum, tensions arise when the group slows down to engage the new people and help them to be productive. This part of the process is called *onboarding.*

But while onboarding generates strain, it can also bring many benefits. As part of the process, you'll need to work with your group to refine your pitch and vision, which should lead to an inspection and refinement of the foundations of your shared understanding. And as you interact with new participants, they'll shed light on aspects of your collaboration that you haven't yet fully considered. They'll prompt you to improve your ideas, approaches and shared capability, even before they've begun to work with you.

At least, this happens when onboarding goes well. If you don't take this part of collaboration seriously, giving it the attention and resourcing it deserves, it can result in tensions that overwhelm a group's ability to resolve them. For example, having would-be participants tear holes in your ideas before they fully understand what you are trying to achieve can be demoralising and deflating, which can kill your momentum, and even your collaboration.

This tool is designed to help you get your onboarding approach together, to work out how to do it so that it suits your growth ambitions. You need the right level of information and engagement so that your prospective participants can understand and connect with your vision quickly, as well as seeing their value proposition for participation. You must also accommodate their participation and integrate their contributions, which means different things for different collaborations. Finally, keep improving your ability to onboard, as you'll have to do it over and over again until you meet your growth goals.

STEP 1: ASSESS THE NEED FOR SCALABILITY OF ONBOARDING

Look at the lists you compiled as part of step 2 in Tool 33: A Growth Assessment. Count of how many participants this generated for each of your 3Cs lists and compare it with the back-of-an-envelope count you did as part of step 2 in Tool 32: The Golden Staircase. Use both counts to arrive at new numbers for each of the 3Cs that inspire excitement and confidence in your group. These three lists should cover all participants for the lifetime of your collaboration.

Next, try to sequence how these participants will be onboarded, accounting for the total number of participants for each period, in each stream (see Table 5 for a simple presentation).

Feel free to use any timeline that seems appropriate, in terms of overall duration as well as what length of period you use.

	January-March	April-June	July-September	October-November
Core	3	5	6	6
Community	0	2	6	3
Crowd	10	15	100	200

Table 5. Sample Onboarding Count

This approach allows you to quickly assess what you're going to face in terms of onboarding. From Table 5, which relates to my current music project, I can see that I'll need to ramp up the onboarding from July onwards. I can also see that the main challenge is not really in the core or the community but more the crowd. My community shrinks in the fourth quarter, as much of that expertise is required for the earlier production of recordings and initial launch materials (which will become inputs for the onboarding of the crowd). These sorts of expansions and contractions of your 3Cs stakeholders are to be expected, so anticipate what this might look like for your own collaboration.

Use the table you created to assess how scalable your onboarding processes need to be for each of the 3Cs. That is, in which of these areas will you most have to address the need to bring in more people: in your core, community or crowd, or combinations thereof?

STEP 2: ASSESS THE INPUTS FOR ONBOARDING

Using the plotting of your onboarding needs from step 1, consider how much onboarding will happen and in what timeframes. The more onboarding that needs to happen in less time, the more your onboarding process and all that goes into it will need to work independently of human effort; that is, the more content and technology you'll need to support it. Conversely, if you have more time, you can do more using face-to-face, phone and other types of human-powered interaction – although, while these will give you greater depth of engagement and potentially higher conversion rates regarding your prospective participants, they can only scale so far, so fast.

If you're considering onboarding more than a dozen folks within a month or so, you'll be in the territory of needing greater content and technology support. In the first instance, this can be in the form of written materials that help you communicate your ideas and the value proposition for participation. But as the number of new participants increases, or the time for onboarding shortens, you'll need to work harder to support their awareness of the collaboration opportunity, provide access to this communication content, and get them involved.

Independent of the numbers you want to onboard, and when you want to do this, each collaboration will have different onboarding needs depending on its subject matter, participants and setting. The level of formality is one major consideration. Try to match it with your onboarding approach and your collaboration setting. A boardroom-style presentation followed by a hard ask will probably come off as pushy in more-informal community or artistic collaborations. On the other hand, if your collaboration is taking place within a professional setting, you'll get better results by getting to the point quickly regarding what's in it for the participants and what their commitment needs to be.

Irrespective of your setting, I recommend having some written and/or graphical resources to support the onboarding, even if these are just notes to keep you focused during a conversation. More often than not, you'll benefit from having a one-pager on the opportunity to be shared, or a slide deck to support a presentation. If you completed Tool 14: The Why–How–What Discussion, then you'll already have a version of this for bringing together your core participants.

To determine your onboarding inputs, use the results from step 1 (number of people and timing of the onboarding), along with your activity plan from Tool 33. Consider what content will serve you best, things like talking points, one-pagers, presentations, videos and website content. You also need to think about how this content will reach people, specifically the channels for its delivery; for example, meetings and presentations, phone calls, email, social media, websites and the like.

With your step 1 results and activity plan before you, make a list of the pieces of content that will best serve your needs at key points of the onboarding. At the same time, add to this list the method of delivery of specific pieces of content. Do this for your core, community and crowd, perhaps for different periods of time for each to suit what you're planning. Your list might end up looking something like Table 6.

Core Onboarding Inputs	
Content	Delivery
Project concept one-pager	Email
Presentation slides	Participant workshop
Website copy	Project website

Table 6. Sample Onboarding Inputs

The idea here is to do your best to be realistic about what you'll need, beyond human interaction, to support the process of attracting and successfully onboarding participants, in line with your vision.

STEP 3: ITERATE FOR IMPROVEMENT

The final step in this tool is designed to improve your onboarding capability as you deliver it. This can be as simple as taking the time after a given onboarding activity to consider what could have worked better, then making the relevant improvements. Ideally, get feedback directly from those with whom you're engaging.

Brainstorm simple ways in which you can get different perspectives on how well you communicated your ideas and how well the channels of delivery met the needs of those you engaged. Build this step into your plans so that it isn't missed. The better the feedback and the sooner you integrate it, the more likely your onboarding efforts will fulfil your growth ambitions.

Another consideration for improving onboarding as you go is understanding when the process is finished, or in other words, what success looks like. This isn't always as straightforward as it might seem, because exactly when someone is 'in your collaboration' and 'successfully collaborating' are highly subjective notions. They'll also vary depending on whether they're being onboarded into your core, community or crowd.

Do your best to gauge when the onboarding has been done by writing down a simple description of what you think successful onboarding looks like. Do this for the core, community and crowd, as it's relevant to your growth plans and the overall initiative. The end result might look something like this:

Participants have been successfully onboarded to the core, when they've turned up to several regular work sessions and are meaningfully contributing to the work and discussions.

Participants have been successfully onboarded to the community, when an agreement has been reached on the delivery of their services.

Participants have been successfully onboarded to the crowd, when they've signed up to our newsletter.

Equipped with these defined end points, make a plan for when to collect feedback for the improvement of your onboarding process and the materials and channels involved.

Tool 35: A 3Cs Analysis of Technologies for Growth

I don't know how many times I've been asked, 'What's the best collaboration software?' My answer is always, 'It depends'. This takes us all the way back to one of the first ideas explored in this book: that while I know what collaboration means, and so do you, *we* don't. Without a commonly shared definition and understanding of what collaboration means and how it works, we can't even begin to have a meaningful conversation about what the best technology might be for an initiative.

This is the purpose of the three principles of collaboration, especially the 3Cs framework of the second principle (shared process) – providing a common language and understanding for use in such a conversation. The technical definitions of each of the 3Cs delineate the activities that will drive your specific collaboration, as well as the software features needed to support those activities. The 3Cs make it possible to answer questions like, 'We want our participants to cocreate a vision statement online. Does this software have the features to support this?'

Formulating and answering questions like this is exactly what we'll do through this tool. Then, once you have a particular technology in mind, we'll go a step further to consider what the challenges for adoption will be and how to plan for them.

STEP 1: IDENTIFY THE ACTIVITIES THAT TECHNOLOGY NEEDS TO SUPPORT

Take a moment to recall the definitions of *cocreation, cooperation and coordination* (see Figure 14). If you need a refresher, revisit the second

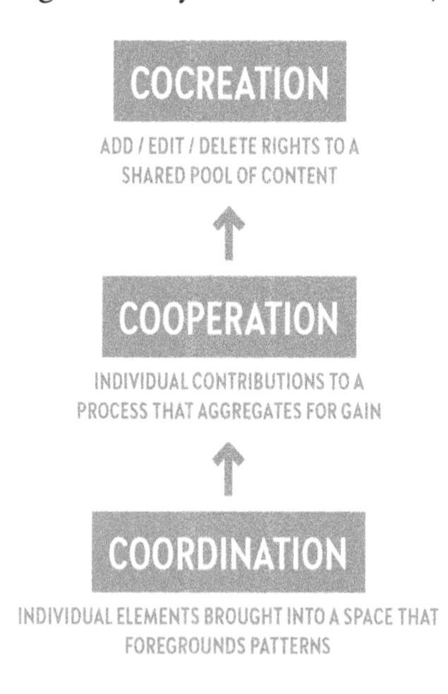

Figure 14. The 3Cs of Collaboration: Cocreation, Cooperation and Coordination

principle of collaboration – shared process – in Chapter 6. Next, revisit your outputs from steps 2 and 3 of Tool 33: A Growth Assessment. Look at the list of participants for each of the 3Cs, as well as the activities you have planned for them. Write down the key activities that you see for each of the lists (see Table 7). There can be more than one activity for each of the 3Cs, or none if you see no role for technology. The activities should sit relatively comfortably under the definitions of the 3Cs.

For example, if you have the activity 'Contribute to co-authoring a section of the strategy document', then this clearly fits under cocreation, while 'Contribute to a survey that identifies key interests for the strategy' would sit under cooperation. This new list of activities is not so much about the people listed in your stakeholder map but rather the activities that you need to support the outputs they'll produce, irrespective of who is producing them.

3Cs	Activity
Coordination	First point of contact and direct to landing point
	Landing point with onboarding info and links to all opportunities for activity
	Subscribe to and receive newsletter
Cooperation	Contribute to a survey that identifies key interests for the strategy
Cocreation	Contribute to co-authoring a section of the strategy document

Table 7. Sample 3Cs Activity List

So feel free to ignore the stakeholder groups or individuals for this tool – just stay focused on collecting all of the activities under each of the 3Cs.

STEP 2: MAP THE ACTIVITIES TO TECHNOLOGY FEATURES

Now build out this table by creating a simple user journey, comprising the touchpoints that a user will have with your technology (see

Table 8). This journey is essentially a step-by-step ordering of how a user will arrive at and move from one activity to another. Also add a column for candidate technologies that have the features to support your activities.

3Cs	Journey Touchpoint and Activity	Technology
Coordination	Touchpoint 1 First point of contact and direct to landing point	Twitter, Facebook, Instagram?
	Touchpoint 2 Landing point with onboarding info and links to all opportunities for activity	Website
	Touchpoint 3 Subscribe to newsletter	Mailchimp
Cooperation	Touchpoint 4 Contribute to a survey that identifies key interests for the strategy	SurveyMonkey
Cocreation	Touchpoint 5 Contribute to co-authoring a section of the strategy document	Google Docs or a wiki?

Table 8. Sample 3Cs Activity List with Touchpoints and Technologies

Try not to get stuck trying to decide which of the 3Cs a particular activity should sit in. The distinction is often blurry. It's far more important that you give it enough thought to be able to match it to a software feature. Just make your best guess.

When adding technology platforms, you aren't coming to any final conclusions here either, just identifying the options, so feel free to add more than one if you're tossing up a few. If you don't know any, do some simple web research. Another good approach is to ask the people around you about technologies they're aware of that might meet your needs. You probably won't need anything too sophisticated, so your friends and peers should be able to give you some pointers. And if you have kids, especially teenagers, ask them too, as they might have some experience or knowledge of whatever you're considering.

If what you need is fairly sophisticated – meaning it's beyond any off-the-shelf tools – then work out what a simpler version might be, or how to take just the first step with a pre-existing technology as a way of informing your decision. Most new custom technologies cost a great deal of money to create, and they don't always satisfy the user's needs or interests. So be very wary of producing anything new to support your collaboration. If you are considering this path, make sure you're focused on developing prototypes as soon as possible to confirm your assumptions about what you need.

As I mentioned earlier, *adoption* is typically the biggest hurdle for making effective use of technology in collaboration. Step 3 will help you work out which options are strong candidates for acceptance by your participants, irrespective of their features or functionality.

STEP 3: ASSESS ADOPTION FRICTION

Show the table you completed in step 2 of this tool to the core. Hopefully you've already introduced the 3Cs to them, but if not, do so now. Once they understand the rationale for organising the information this way – activities that align with the 3Cs, as well as the user journey – discuss the technologies that you've listed.

Find out if the members of your cocreating core have any experience in using the proposed technologies. If so, talk about what those experiences were like and if the core group feels that the technology would be a good fit for the proposed activity. If they haven't actually used them, discuss their attitudes towards these technologies. Have they heard of them? Would they be open to trying them? How do they think your proposed participants will view the technology choices?

It's surprising how often people have preconceived ideas and strong opinions about particular technologies, even if they've never used them. For example, a person may see Instagram as something that's appropriate for kids, but not for the more serious nature of their particular collaboration, completely independent of whether it has the right features and best user experience of the technologies available. These attitudes are very important to note, though, because they are likely indicative of how your potential participants may feel, and the likelihood of them having a go. In essence, these attitudes reflect the user base that has been attracted to a technology through social proof by a particular demographic. This doesn't mean you shouldn't use a given technology if negative attitudes about it are present and its use is dominated by a demographic that's different to those you're looking to engage, but you'll certainly need to do extra work to overcome these issues.

Now try to find out if your *prospective* participants already use the proposed technologies. Sometimes, a little online 'stalking' will get you the information you seek. For example, pick a proposed or representative participant and see if they have an account on the platform you're looking at. This may not be possible with technologies whose use is not public (for example, Google Docs) or if users have made their profiles private. In these cases, you may be able to reach out directly to them, to ask about their experiences and opinions.

Getting direct input from your prospective participants is the gold standard to aim for, but if this isn't possible, use your own experience as a proxy. Give the technologies you're considering a try to get a feel for what they're like, especially in creating an account and logging in for the first time, which is usually where the most friction occurs. Develop a plan to test all the technologies in this way before committing to them.

As you do this, try to see your experience through the eyes of your hopeful users. Identify the pain-points they're likely to have and plan to support these. Most technology platforms these days have decent support already available, in the form of FAQs, videos, chatbots and so on. You can make use of these to create a streamlined resource for participants, quickly pointing them to the most relevant support.

After the discussions with your core, create a final version of the user journey, along with the activities and supporting technologies you'll try. Now you can create a plan for confirming and testing the technologies, as well as creating the content and support materials allowing participants to navigate and adopt them. Keep in mind your onboarding process, especially when and where this is taking place in the user journey. You should also plan to update and revise your content, your process, and potentially even your technology choices, in line with the plan for iteratively improving the onboarding experience that you developed using Tool 34: Onboarding Participants.

Tool 36: When to Stop Collaborating

The social bonds and collective commitment required for successful collaboration can make it hard for a group to stop when the time comes, so it can be particularly difficult to recognise when this time has come. In fact, it's different for each collaborative situation. For more outcomes-focused collaborations, there will be a clear 'Job done!' moment. Other initiatives will be open-ended, with no clear finish line in sight – ever. And then there's everything in-between.

For collaborations that lack a concrete completion point, there are no formulas or rules for when to stop, but nonetheless, at some point you'll probably feel that this is necessary. There will be a nagging irritation somewhere deep inside you. You may find yourself getting unreasonably annoyed by the normal challenges that collaboration presents, or by the quirks or foibles of your peers. It may also just begin to feel like a painful chore, when previously it was the highlight of your week. Irrespective, in my experience it's best to make this decision consciously and explicitly, rather than letting the initiative fizzle away into nothing, with the participants simply drifting off.

If you suspect that you may have done your dash with a particular group or initiative, take some time to reflect on the situation by asking yourself these questions:

1 Do I lack the inspiration and motivation to contribute my best? If so, what would it take to gain this? Is this possible or realistic?
2 Is it possible that my participation is a drag or a drain on anyone else involved? Am I preventing the group from heading in new directions?
3 Is the group preventing me from going in new directions? Am I inspired or excited by the thought of going in different directions than where the group may be able or willing to go?
4 What would I do with the time and energy I'd gain if I left the collaboration? Does having this time and energy get me inspired or excited?

If you answered a solid 'Yes' to many of these questions, you owe it to yourself and your peers to consider and raise with your group the prospect of departing. If you continue to work with your teeth clenched, lacking inspiration, interest and/or motivation, you'll do more harm than good by participating. It will ultimately infect everyone's efforts, bringing the collaboration down or at least reducing its potential.

This doesn't mean you should just walk away the minute you no longer feel the rosy glow of collaborative achievement. Collaboration is hard work that, much of the time, doesn't exactly feel like 'fun'. You should, however, feel inspired by your vision and the prospect of your group realising it. If you can't connect with that vision, or realistically see the outcomes happening, then it's time to reflect. If the vision is solid but there's an issue with your group's ability to realise the stated outcomes, then that can likely be repaired. If you don't believe in the vision, that's a much more serious issue, one that will be much more difficult to repair. Doing so will depend on you and your group's willingness to openly and honestly engage with the issue.

Whatever your situation, take care when making a decision to stay or go. If you do feel you need to make a change, consider discussing this with your core collaborators before making any decisions. Sometimes a conversation can go a long way towards repairing issues that seem unresolvable. But if you do feel you must depart, pick your moment and be as respectful as possible of the feelings of your fellow participants. Make sure you don't leave your peers with a mess or in a bind, or are otherwise being irresponsible about the timing and circumstances of your departure. If your collaboration is healthy, then your peers should support you in looking after your own needs and interests. If they hold your decision against you, this could be a sign that it was a good call after all.

A group's ability to let go of participants gracefully is actually a capability, and an important one for growth. It demonstrates to others that they aren't locked in, and that the group will support the individual participants' interests as much as the collective's.

Conclusion

You are now armed with three principles, six stages and 36 tools for collaboration design – the Collabforge method – and I encourage you to use them all. Collaboration is simply too challenging and complex to leave to chance. In fact, developing and delivering a great collaboration design will take all the discipline, determination and dedication that you can muster. But your reward will be directly proportional to your effort. And through your self-aware actions and intentions, you'll not only improve the chances of success for one collaboration, but your ability to collaborate successfully in the future.

I would like to leave you with two final 'If you do nothing else ...' pieces of advice.

Always Be Present

As you collaborate, keep your awareness focused on the moment unfolding before you. Actively listen when someone speaks, and actively watch their actions – try to understand what they're saying with their words and their body. Be empathetic to those you work with, be curious about their needs and interests. At the same time, maintain a connection with your own needs and interests. Being present also means maintaining an open and improv mindset, so that you're ready to meet whatever may emerge with the fullness of your being.

Stay Focused on Outcomes

Outcomes are the gold of collaboration – it's the prospect of their realisation that drives participation. Outcomes are the real-world impacts you make because of the things you cocreate, the 'What if ...?' foundation of your commitment to collaborate. They are multidimensional, different for each participant, changing through time, which is why being aware of your participants' needs and interests is critical. And because outcomes are so important, you must always look for ways to accelerate your progress towards their realisation. Even a taste of one can make a huge difference to a striving group, revitalising and inspiring their vision and commitment.

Staying focused on outcomes, like being present, is easier said than done. A million and one things will distract you. Competing priorities, complex logistics and social dynamics, insufficient resources, lack of clarity, confusion, having others confront your ideas and ego – these will all challenge you. But don't let your resolve waver. The benefits will be worth it.

A Final Note: Collaboration's Past and Future

For thousands of years, we humans have been collaborating using the tools we've found around us. No doubt in the earliest part of our history, as we sat around fires, we drew designs in the dirt and discussed how to take down big prey, battle an enemy, make a difficult journey or meal, or simply plan the day. This evolved into paintings in caves and clay tablets, which provided more permanence for our visions and ideas, and eventually we started printing and publishing to increase our impact, share our knowledge and coordinate ever-larger collaborations. The factory line and the organisational chart enabled even larger enterprises. Television, social media, wikis, online communities and virtual worlds have continued this evolution, dramatically extending our capability for collaboration.

New technologies have proven to be game-changers for our collaborations, or distractions, depending on the presence and focus on outcomes we bring to our collaboration designs – it was so in the past and it will be so forever more. And as the development of technology continues to accelerate, we will need even greater focus to ensure alignment between the outcomes we're striving for and the activities that will generate them. True, tools and technologies are simply a means to an end – they enable the activities; they are not the outcomes. But because of the role they play in collaboration, and their potential to amplify our goals, we must remain open to what they offer. Often, however, understanding what they offer isn't possible until you experience them yourself. So every once in a while, roll up your sleeves and try out something new and strange. This goes for new workshop methods and social processes as much as for new hardware and software. New technologies and techniques that can add value to collaboration are emerging all the time. We just need to recognise them as such.

If you have kids, or you've spent any amount of time around them, you'll know that the world they're growing up in is very different to that of their parents. Massive multiplayer online collaborative games and virtual worlds are here, and they're here to stay. Kids are now getting as much collaboration training online as they are in the playground, if not more. This is because in these spaces, they not only play, they team up to cocreate (and destroy) their virtual playgrounds. As they do this, they learn how to use collaborative tools that are many orders of sophistication beyond what most of us use in our professional environments.

And as the youth of today become the adults of tomorrow, their expectations of collaboration will only increase. I believe that these expectations are growing faster than the ability of our organisations and governments to satisfy them. This carries with it the risks of lost profits and market share, alienation and disconnection, even losing the social licence to operate, as customers and citizens increasingly see cocreation as a right, if not a responsibility. Organisations of all types are increasingly having to think about the changing expectations of their staff, customers and communities, as well as the opportunities that collaboration offers to deliver value and build connections.

As our workplaces and broader societies change as a result of such expectations and developing technology, there seems to be a growing fear that automation and robots will push us humans out of our jobs. I have no doubt that innovations like artificial intelligence, robotics, virtual and augmented reality, the Internet of Things and automation will continue to dramatically transform the jobs available to us, and the world around us. However, I think that there will always be a need for solutions that we create and deliver together. Even in a sci-fi future where we're wired up to brain-to-brain neural nets and using robotic appendages, there will be a need to establish shared understanding in order to cocreate and realise a shared vision. I don't believe this will ever go away, not as long as humans exist. It will only increase.

When Einstein said that we cannot solve our problems with the same thinking that created them, he was pointing to the fact that we wield a powerful double-edged sword: with every wonderful new cocreation, we also create new wicked problems that are beyond our current capability to solve and require collaboration to cut through; for example, as we create smartphones and other fantastic technologies, we also create climate change.

What's the takeaway here?

Building your capability to collaborate well will only increase your personal and professional relevance and job security in the world of the future.

Even if you aren't currently looking to create the next great disruptive product, or solve the world's most pressing problems, I can say with confidence that you have personal dreams that are as yet unrealised. I can also say with confidence that your chances of success are greater with effective collaboration. Whether it's launching a new enterprise, a rocket, or a book, virtually every dream worth pursuing requires, or can be enhanced by, collaboration.

I now encourage you to revisit your dreams, while keeping in mind the enormous potential of collaboration design. Beyond what any other people might bring to your dreams, there's nothing quite like the magic of having the third hand show up to help out.

Afterword

One of my own as yet unrealised dreams is for collaboration design to be the subject of many, even competing methodologies that collaborators can choose from. Not only is a little competition healthy, I believe that different collaboration methodologies are actually necessary to address different settings, such as work, home and community, and art, science and health – settings that demand different techniques to get great results. I also believe that these different methods can be linked by common theories, like the three principles of collaboration, which inform the deeper instinct we all have to collaborate.

So here is my ask. If you are passionate about getting the most out of collaboration, about seeing what it has to offer the world, please share your knowledge and experience. Share it with those you are collaborating with. Share it with those around you. Share it with me.

I want you involved because I can only address one small portion of collaboration through my experience and opportunities. I need your input and insights to do much more. For one thing, I need more methods for the different settings in which I must collaborate to realise more of my own dreams – having four precocious boys, I would love to have a method for family collaboration in the home!

I also think you'll benefit from further involvement by getting input and advice about your own efforts from other experts, like me. You might also find that it's fun to connect with like-minded individuals. You might even discover new collaboration opportunities with which to test your own methods and techniques, or to realise those dreams of yours.

Hopefully you've recognised the double-sided value proposition that's at work here. If the idea of collaborating to build ever-better methods of collaboration appeals to you, then get in touch:

collaborate@collabforge.com
twitter.com/collabforge
facebook.com/collabforge

Acknowledgements

This book has its origins in my PhD, which I started all the way back in 2004. The theories and ideas that make up a good part of Part I were the direct result of some fantastic poking and prodding by my supervisors, Elizabeth Presa and Sean Cubitt. I am particularly indebted to Elizabeth, who asked me, 'You keep using that word, collaboration. What do you really mean by it?' She then supported me even as I brought into our meetings stacks of books from every field imaginable and created my 'spaghetti diagrams' to make sense of it all. She also encouraged me to reach out into the big wide world to find kindred spirits, and in doing so I found Howard Rheingold, who has been an inspiration and mentor through it all. He immediately grasped the notion of a general theory of collaboration (and how ants made the theory work!) when many others didn't quite get what I was on about. Thank you Howard.

The method in Part II, however, was developed through hard work in the trenches of the public sector with my fantastic team at Collabforge. Specifically, without the daily support and collaborative efforts of Hailey Cooperrider, I'm sure this method would not exist. Hailey's efforts to help create and share the dream for a method that actually works, ultimately brought this book to life. And her relentless focus on learning and discovering new ideas and techniques, even as I was often stubborn and slow to accept them, kept it evolving. Keep dreaming Hailey – Cheng Ho!

But it was Collabforge's steady stream of dedicated, passionate and visionary innovator public servants who provided the opportunity to develop, apply and refine our methods over the last decade. Through their trust and belief in the power of collaboration, we have had the incredible experience of working together to improve one of the core elements of the operating system of our society – the governance by which our democracy is delivered. Of special note is David Mayes, who discovered my research blog and PhD wiki as I was still completing it, and gave me the opportunity to try out my ideas for real. His vision for, and commitment to, the genuinely collaborative cocreation of an Australian capital city's 10-year strategic plan is still years ahead of its time. Even now, I marvel at how he made that happen, and how, in doing so, he brought into the world all that Collabforge has had the good fortune to experience and achieve. Thank you David!

The actual production of this book (an endeavour I started and stalled at least three times!) would not have been possible without the guidance and gentle whip-cracking of Paul Smitz. His coaching and then editing has made this book many times better than it would have been otherwise (and thank you Shawn Callahan for introducing me to Paul!). Rebecca Dahl's constant reiteration that this book was needed (years ago!) was essential to its creation. Her incredible efforts to help me make the time to write it by doing many of the other things that needed doing, and then to finish the many tasks required once the writing was complete, made it's completed form possible.

The greatest acknowledgement and gratitude must go to Keri Christensen, with whom I collaborate in all things, in life and love. Her belief, support and sacrifice, and her collaborative partnership in making Collabforge the success that it has been, created the platform that made all this possible. And lastly, thank you Cedar, Lucas, Jasper and River, my crazy boyz who help me every day to better understand and appreciate the potential that collaboration presents to us all in creating and realising our dreams.

Index

Page numbers followed by '*i*' indicate an illustration; page numbers followed by '*n*' indicate a footnote.

About the Author

Mark Elliott is a sought-after keynote speaker, author and consultant. In 2007, after finishing his PhD, Mark founded Collabforge, a firm that specialises in helping organisations turn their collaboration challenges into high-impact innovation opportunities. Mark has led Collabforge in delivering over 500 projects with Australian and international government agencies and universities.

Mark has published and delivered keynote presentations on his work to the United Nations, federal governments, international think tanks, and academic and professional conferences around the world. Mark is also a performing musician and composer, having worked collaboratively as an artist his whole life. He has played in countless bands, written works for orchestras and ensembles, and performed in experimental improv groups.

Mark now lives in Melbourne, Australia with his wife and four high-energy boys.

Ingram Content Group UK Ltd.
Milton Keynes UK
UKHW022127060323
418148UK00016B/508/J